D1030344

JAMES FENIMORE COOPER

BY

W. B. SHUBRICK CLYMER

J. Fenimore Cooper

JAMES FENIMORE COOPER

BY

W. B. SHUBRICK CLYMER

HASKELL HOUSE PUBLISHERS Ltd.
Publishers of Scarce Scholarly Books
NEW YORK, N. Y. 10012
1968

First Published 1900

HASKELL HOUSE PUBLISHERS LTD.
Publishers of Scarce Scholarly Books
280 LAFAYETTE STREET
NEW YORK, N. Y. 10012

Library of Congress Catalog Card Number: 68-24933

Haskell House Catalogue Item # 925

Printed in the United States of America

The photogravure used as a frontispiece to this volume is after an engraving of a daguerreotype taken by Brady in 1850. The present engraving is by John Andrew & Son, Boston.

To the Memory

of

WILLIAM BRANFORD SHUBRICK

U. S. N.

PREFACE.

It is sixty years since Irving closed "The Pathfinder" with the gracious words: "They may say what they will of Cooper: the man who wrote this book is not only a great man, but a good man." There is not a doubt of it. Study of his life teaches that evil tongues need not blight fair fame. Bryant, in the memorial address delivered five months after Cooper's death, told simple truth which the world now accepts. Professor Lounsbury thirty years later demonstrated, by critical sifting of all the published evidence, that in agreeing with Irving and Bryant the world is right.

Shortly stating the most significant facts, yet omitting so much relevant matter as at times to endanger narrative continuity, I have followed, with the incidental aid of literary histories and the like, and with some personal help from friends, the able guidance of the only biographer of Cooper. My indebtedness to him is interlined on al-

most every page of this tiny volume, for which no claim is made except that certain hitherto unpublished letters, placed in my hands by kind fortune, here and there enable Cooper to speak for himself.

W. B. S. C.

BOSTON, June 23, 1900.

CHRONOLOGY.

1789

September 15. James [Fenimore] Cooper was born at Burlington, New Jersey.

1790

October 10. His father brought his family to Cooperstown, on Otsego Lake, in the State of New York, where he built, between 1796 and 1799, Otsego Hall.

1799

Became a private pupil of the rector of St. Peter's Church in Albany.

1803

Entered the freshman class at Yale College.

1805

Was dismissed from college.

1806–1807

Served for eleven months before the mast aboard the *Sterling*.

1808

January 1. Received commission as midshipman in the United States navy.

1808 (*continued*)

Served on board the *Vesuvius*.

Was one of a party sent to Oswego, on Lake Ontario, to build the brig *Oneida* during the winter of 1808–1809.

1809

Was attached to the *Wasp*, Captain James Lawrence.

December. His father died.

1810

May 9. Was granted a furlough of twelve months.

1811

January 1. Was married at Mamaroneck, Westchester County, New York, to Susan Augusta de Lancey.

May 6. Resigned from the navy on the expiration of his furlough.

Lived with his wife's family at Mamaroneck.

1813–1817

Lived for a short time at Cooperstown, afterward at Fenimore.

1817

Returned to Mamaroneck. His mother died at Otsego Hall. Went to live at Scarsdale.

1820

Published *Precaution* anonymously.

1821

Published *The Spy* anonymously.

1822

Removed to New York.

1823

April 18. Was made a member of the American Philosophical Society, of Philadelphia.

Published *The Pioneers*, *Tales for Fifteen*, and *The Pilot*, though the last did not actually appear until January of the following year.

1824

Received from Columbia College the degree of Master of Arts.

1825

Published *Lionel Lincoln*.

1826

Published *The Last of the Mohicans.*

April. His name was changed, by act of Legislature, to Fenimore-Cooper.

May 10. Was appointed consul at Lyons.

June 1. Sailed from New York, with his family, for Europe. Lived in and near Paris for a year and a half.

1827

Published *The Prairie.*

1828

Published *The Red Rover.* Passed four months in England. Travelled in Holland, Belgium, France, Switzerland, and Italy. Published *Notions of the Americans.*

1829

Relinquished consulship at Lyons.

Published *The Wept of Wish-ton-Wish.*

December. Went to Rome for the winter.

1830

April. Left Rome.

June. Reached Dresden, where *The Water Witch* was published.

1830 (*continued*)

July. Went to Paris on the outbreak of the Revolution, and lived there during the greater part of the next three years.

1831

Published *The Bravo.*

1832

Published *The Heidenmauer.*

1833

Published *The Headsman.*

November 5. Landed in New York, after an absence abroad of seven years and five months.

1834

Renovated Otsego Hall, which subsequently became his permanent residence. Published *A Letter to His Countrymen.*

1835

Published *The Monikins.*

1836

Published *Sketches of Switzerland.*

1837

Published *Gleanings in Europe* (France, England). Three Mile Point controversy, followed by suits for libel.

1838

Published *Gleanings in Europe* (Italy), *The American Democrat*, *The Chronicles of Cooperstown*, *Homeward Bound*, and *Home as Found.*

1839

May 10. Published *The History of the Navy of the United States of America.*
July 8. Was made a member of the Georgia Historical Society.

1840

Published *The Pathfinder* and *Mercedes of Castile.*

1841

Published *The Deerslayer.*

1842

Published *The Two Admirals.*
Engaged to write regularly for *Graham's Magazine.*

1842 (*continued*)

June 16. Decision was rendered by the arbitrators in the matter of the *Naval History*.

Published *The Wing-and-Wing*.

1843

Published *The Autobiography of a Pocket Handkerchief* (in *Graham's Magazine*), *The Battle of Lake Erie*, *Wyandotte*, and *Ned Myers*.

1844

Published *Afloat and Ashore*, *Proceedings of the Naval Court Martial in the Case of Alexander Slidell Mackenzie*, and *Miles Wallingford*.

June 6. Was made a member of the Maryland Historical Society.

1845

Published *Satanstoe*.

1846

Published *The Chainbearer*, *Lives of Distinguished American Naval Officers*

1846 (*continued*)

(previously contributed to *Graham's Magazine*), and *The Redskins.*

1847

Published *The Crater.*

1848

Published *Jack Tier* (which had appeared serially in *Graham's Magazine*) and *The Oak Openings.*

1849

Published *The Sea Lions.*

1850

Published *The Ways of the Hour.*

June 18. *Upside Down; or, Philosophy in Petticoats,* a comedy, was produced by Burton.

1851

July. Confirmed in the Protestant Episcopal Church.

September 14. James Fenimore Cooper died at Cooperstown.

JAMES FENIMORE COOPER

JAMES FENIMORE COOPER.

I.

THERE came to America in 1679 one James Cooper. In the deeds showing his purchase, four years later, of two tracts of land from the proprietors of West New Jersey, he is referred to as of Stratford-on-Avon; and in certain conveyances of parcels of land subsequently purchased in Philadelphia, as a merchant. Owning a considerable amount of real estate in New Jersey and Pennsylvania, and presumably succeeding in business, he is believed to have become a man of some importance among the Quakers. Of the family of his first wife, whom he married probably after coming to this country, not even the name survives. Their descendants appear to have been well-to-do farmers.

Among them was William Cooper, who was born in Byberry township, Pennsylvania, seventy-five years after his ancestor's arrival in this country. In 1775 he married, at Burlington, New Jersey, Elizabeth, only child of Richard Fenimore, who was descended from early English settlers in New Jersey, in which province the Fenimores held several offices. Both William Cooper and his wife were Quakers. He became interested, soon after the Revolution, in large tracts of land in New York and elsewhere. His character, as well as the nature of the country where his illustrious son's infancy and childhood were passed, is best shown in some letters he wrote to a friend who had been exiled from Ireland and had taken up the practice of the law in New York. Beginning with a small capital and a large family, he had settled, he writes about 1805, "more acres than any man in America. . . . In 1785 I visited the rough and hilly country of Otsego, where there existed not an inhabitant nor any trace of a road. I was alone, three hundred miles from home, without bread, meat, or food of any kind. . . . My horse fed on the grass that grew by the edge of the waters. I laid me down to sleep in my watch-coat, nothing but the melancholy wilderness around me." At the outlet of Otsego Lake, the source of the Susquehanna, where for a century Indian traders had been accustomed to resort, and of which the name is supposed to signify such a meeting-place, he laid out in 1787 a village called Coopers-Town; and thither he brought his family in 1790. "This was the first settlement I made, and the first attempted after the Revolution." His success in the difficult enterprise he attributes to a "steady mind, a sober judgment, fortitude, perseverance, and, above all, common sense." After years of privation and hardship, in 1796 contracts were made for the construction of Otsego Hall, where the wise and just landlord lived among the community which he had founded. For nine years he was first judge of the County Court of Common Pleas, and he served two terms in Congress. An ardent politician, in close relations with the Federalist leaders, he took an active part in the heated contests of those critical times when the North American republic was in its infancy.

On September 15, 1789, the eleventh of William and Elizabeth Fenimore Cooper's twelve children was born at Burlington, New Jersey. He was called for his grandfather, whose name was that of the ancestor who had migrated from Stratford; and until he was past thirty-six his full name was James Cooper. While he was still a boy, his mother, on the extinction of the male line in her family, had expressed a wish that one of her children should take her surname, promising in return to leave such child her real estate in the neighbourhood of Cooperstown. Her husband had objected; but James, the youngest of seven children then surviving, had offered to do as his mother requested. Long after both parents were dead, he accordingly petitioned for leave to change his surname to Fenimore, intending that his name should be James Cooper Fenimore. But the legislature made the surname Fenimore-Cooper. Though protesting that that was not what he had asked for, he adopted the name in that form; and so for a time he occasionally wrote it.

The removal from his birthplace to Cooperstown when he was but thirteen months old, and the establishment there of the family residence, identify him with the State of New York. Of his childhood little is told, except that he lived healthily and naturally, surrounded by out-of-door influences which did much to direct his tastes and to shape his character. For the growth of innate self-reliance and purity of heart, dominant traits inherited from his Quaker parents, it would have been hard to find a soil more favourable than the young community of which his father was the founder and the leader. From an elder sister, who died in 1800 in consequence of a fall from a horse, and whose memory was always cherished with peculiar tenderness by her brother, the boy received his earliest instruction.

Among a number of apocryphal anecdotes about Cooper is one related by Hawthorne, who tells of Bryant's saying he had heard Cooper speak of having held a successful spiritual communication with this sister after her death. The story is mentioned here only to give an opportunity to correct a current impression that Cooper believed in Spiritualism. There is ample evidence that such was not the case, but that his only interest in the subject was an amused curiosity as to the means by which the manifestations were produced.

The next step from his sister's tuition was to "Master" Cory's village "Academy." Thence he went, at nine, to Albany, to be for four years a pupil of the rector of St. Peter's Church, the son of a beneficed English clergyman, a graduate of Oxford, and a man of scholarship, who entertained, according to a lively reminiscent sketch drawn by Cooper many years later, "a most profound reverence for the king and the nobility; was not backward in expressing his contempt for all classes of dissenters and all ungentlemanly sects; was particularly severe on the immoralities of the French Revolution, and, though eating our bread, was not especially lenient to our own; . . . spent his money freely, and sometimes that of other people; was particularly tenacious of the ritual and of all the decencies of the Church; detested a democrat as he did the devil; . . . prayed fervently on Sundays; decried all morals, institutions, churches, manners, and laws but those of England Mondays and Saturdays; and, as it subsequently became known, was living every day in the week, *in vinculo matrimonii*, with another man's wife!"

The death of this accomplished gentleman in 1802 sent his pupil prematurely to Yale when a mere stripling of thirteen, by only two weeks the senior of the youngest student in college, the poet Hillhouse. Like many another well-prepared, clever boy of truant disposition before and since, Cooper, when left to follow his bent, neglected his books, and learned more about the pretty surroundings of New Haven than about Greek and Latin. "But the study of scenery," as his biographer appositely remarks, "however desirable in itself, cannot easily be included in a college curriculum." In his third year, therefore, the authorities, with President Dwight at their head, saw no reason, despite his father's remonstrance, for not punishing him by dismissal for being engaged in some bit of boyish mischief which they disapproved of. Had he attended to his work and taken his degree, which Yale never in later years saw fit to honour herself by giving him, the chances are that his novels, while losing none of the benefit they undoubtedly derived from his rambles in the country, would have gained in style. Columbia, in this instance more intelligent than either Yale or Harvard, in 1824 conferred on him the honorary degree of A.M.

Judge Cooper chose the navy as the most promising opening for his independent and adventurous son, who was accordingly, as a preliminary step, sent to sea before the mast in a merchantman. That was the fashion of the day, when there was no Naval Academy, "though its utility," as Cooper sensibly says, "on the whole, may very well be questioned."

An animated account of his eleven months' experience aboard the *Sterling*, "one of the wettest ships that ever floated, when heading up against the sea," is given in *Ned Myers*, which is the true story of the life of a shipmate on this first voyage, who, after passing some twenty-five years out of sight of land, turned up at Cooperstown in 1843, and spun the yarn which Cooper wove into a book. The *Sterling* was commanded by a young Maine man who was "kind and considerate in his treatment of all hands"; and she carried a motley crew, comprising, besides Americans, a Portuguese, a Spaniard, a Prussian, a Dane, an Englishman, a Scotch boy, and a Canadian. After a stormy voyage of some forty days from New York, "during which the ship was on a bow-line most of the time," they anchored in St. Helen's Roads, and thence went up to London to discharge cargo. "I had one or two cruises of a Sunday," says Myers, "in tow of Cooper, who soon became a branch pilot in those waters, about the parks and west end. . . . Most of us went to see the monument, St. Paul's, and the lions; and Cooper put himself in charge of a beef-eater, and took a look at the arsenals, jewels, and armoury. He had a rum time of it, in his sailor rig, but hoisted in a wonderful lot of gibberish, according to his own account of the cruise." The following January the *Sterling* had a stormy passage to the Straits of Gibraltar, was saved by an English frigate from a Portuguese pirate, and narrowly escaped being run down by a man-of-war. She had rough weather again, and ran short of provisions, on the return voyage to London. There she remained for two or three months, not sailing for Philadelphia until the end of July. It is of this homeward voyage that Cooper afterward wrote: "I have myself been one of eleven hands, officers included, to navigate a ship of near three hundred tons across the Atlantic Ocean; and, what is more, we often reefed topsails with the watch." Fifty-two days of storm and adventure brought the *Sterling* safe, at last, to port on September 18, 1807. Such was the first taste of salt water of the eighteen-year-old boy who at thirty-four gave to the world the first tale of the sea since Smollett's *Roderick Random*.

Cooper entered the navy as a midshipman on January 1, 1808. During the next three years he saw a fair amount of service. The part of it most important in result was a trip to Lake Ontario, to build the *Oneida*, a brig of sixteen guns, intended for use in the war which then threatened with England. The experiences of the winter at Oswego (1808–9), related in Cooper's biographical notice of Woolsey, who commanded the expedition, were used more than thirty years afterward in *The Pathfinder*. In 1809, after a visit with Woolsey to Niagara Falls, Cooper was left with the gunboats on Lake Champlain. In the same year he was attached to the *Wasp*, under Captain Lawrence, a native of Burlington and a personal friend, the heroic commander of the *Chesapeake* in her action with the *Shannon*. On board the *Wasp* began a lifelong friendship with Shubrick, of South Carolina, a midshipman like himself, and his junior by one year, to whom he dedicated *The Pilot* and *The Red Rover*.

In December of 1809 Judge Cooper was knocked on the head by an opponent, after a political meeting in Albany, and died from the effect of the blow.

To the eldest son, Richard, thus left head of the family, James writes as follows from New York on May 18, 1810: "When you were in the city, I hinted to you my intention of resigning at the end of this session of Congress, should nothing be done for the navy. My only reason at that time was the blasted prospects of the service. I accordingly wrote my resignation, and, as usual, offered it to Captain Lawrence for his inspection. He very warmly recommended to me to give the service the trial of another year or two, at the same time offering to procure me a furlough which would leave me perfect master of my actions in the interval. I thought it wisest to accept this proposition. At the end of this year I have it in my power to resign, should the situation of the country warrant it." He goes on to say that he has met Miss de Lancey, and asked her to marry him; and he requests his brother to write to her father, approving of the match.

John Peter de Lancey — whose Huguenot grandfather, Étienne, had fled from Normandy on the revocation of the Edict of Nantes, and in 1686 had come to New York — was the fourth son of James, Chief Justice and Lieutenant-

Governor of New York, and of his wife Anne, eldest daughter of Hon. Caleb Heathcote, Lord of the Manor of Scarsdale. Born in New York, and educated at Harrow and in the Military School at Greenwich, he entered the army, and became a captain in an Irish regiment. After serving in a Loyalist regiment during the Revolution, he returned to England, left the army, and married Elizabeth, daughter of Colonel Richard Floyd, of Long Island. With her he came back to Westchester County in 1789, and passed the remainder of his life at Heathcote Hill, which he had inherited from his mother, and where he built a house on the site of the old manor house, which had been burned. Here his daughter, Susan Augusta, was born; and here on New Year's Day, 1811, she became Mrs. James Cooper.

Cooper and his young bride began married life auspiciously by playing a game of chess between the ceremony and the supper. Then, "he driving two horses tandem," they made their wedding journey to Cooperstown in a gig. For over forty years their life was in the deepest sense united. She was richly endowed with the gracious feminine faculty of guiding by affection the man who yet controls the household, and he was chivalrously devoted to her. At the expiration of his furlough a few months after the marriage, instead of applying for duty, he carried out his intention, formed a year before, of resigning from the navy. This step pleased her, for she dreaded separation from him. "She confesses," he writes long afterward, "she would never have done for Lady Collingwood."

After a brief essay at housekeeping in a cottage at Mamaroneck so tiny that he called it Closet Hall, the young people returned to live with her family at Heathcote Hill, whence they removed, with their two little girls, to

Fenimore, a small place near Cooperstown. The memories of the next few years are full of charm. On a rising knoll overlooking the lake and village a stone house was begun, in which they expected to pass their lives. Riding, driving, rowing, skating, gardening, playing the flute, Cooper at twenty-five, brave and handsome, pasturing on a hill close by, called Mt. Ovis, the merino sheep which he had introduced into the county, had truly a pleasant calling. He was active, too, as secretary of the County Agricultural Society, and as vestryman of Christ Church and secretary of the Otsego County Bible Society; and he found a few congenial associates among the many European residents of the village. His mother was living at Otsego Hall with his elder brothers. "She took great delight in flowers, and the south end of the long hall was like a greenhouse in her time. She was a great reader of romances. She was a marvellous house-keeper, and beautifully nice, and neat, in all her arrangements. Her flower-garden was at the south of the house, and was considered something wonderful in the variety of flowers."

The first little girl died at Fenimore, and two others were born. And then the family set out, in 1817, for a visit to Heathcote Hill, expecting to return in a few months to the stone house which was still building. But they never lived in it; for it was burned, the property was sold, and the absence of a few months extended to seventeen years. Later in 1817 Cooper's mother died.

They had not been long at Heathcote Hill before it was decided to build a country-house on a farm in Scarsdale, four miles from Mamaroneck, called Angevine—the name of the preceding Huguenot tenants. The situation is described as commanding a "beautiful view over the farms and woods of the adjoining country, in whose varied groves hickory and tulip-tree, cedar and sassafras, grew abundantly," and as overlooking the Sound "always dotted with the white sails the sailor's eye loved to follow in their graceful movements to and fro, while the low shores of Long Island, with the famous pippin orchards of Newtown, formed the distant background." In this attractive spot, Cooper led much the same sort of life as at Fenimore — driving, riding, sailing, reading in a desultory way, and always much interested in gardening and in politics. In 1818 he was appointed paymaster, and the next year quartermaster, in the fourth division of infantry of the New York State Militia. As Governor Clinton's aide, in blue and buff uniform, with cocked hat and sword, and the title of Colonel, he would go to reviews mounted on his favourite horse, "Bull-head."

One evening — the story runs — as he

was reading aloud to Mrs. Cooper a novel which had come from England in the last monthly packet, he impatiently exclaimed, "I could write you a better book myself!" She laughed at the absurd idea that he, who disliked even writing a letter, should write a book. But he was bent on trying, and almost at once began "a tale, not yet named, the scene laid in England, as a matter of course." After writing a few chapters, he was for giving it up; but she urged him to finish it and, to his great amusement, to print it. So it was decided to hear what their friends and neighbours, the Jays, would say. They accordingly set out in the gig for Bedford with the manuscript. The audience approved, one lady, who was not in the secret, feeling sure she had "read it before." After consultation with Charles Wilkes and other friends, *Precaution*, which aimed to imitate the average English story of fashionable life, was published anonymously in 1820. The authorship was attributed to an English lady. Though this first and last attempt of Cooper's to copy any one else now reposes in oblivion beside its nameless model, the publication was yet momentous because it led to the writing of *The Spy*, which was literally the "first brilliantly successful romance published in America."

II.

THE early volumes of Stedman and Hutchinson's *Library of American Literature* conclusively demonstrate the literary sterility of this country during the seventeenth and eighteenth centuries, or (to be precise) between Captain John Smith's *True Relation* (1608) — apocryphally reputed to be the first American book— and the *Wieland* (1798) of Charles Brockden Brown, who is invariably spoken of as the first professional American writer. That interval in England includes all the great literature which appeared between *King Lear* and the *Lyrical Ballads*, whereas the only fact universally known about the writing so copiously produced in America during those years is that its character is fundamentally religious or political, as distinguished from literary. Our Quaker and Puritan ancestors for several generations consecrated their lives to the making of a nation. With the Muses they did not dally overmuch. So it comes about that the first man west of the Atlantic to publish what may fairly be rated as imaginative prose fiction was Brown, and he was alone. In 1845 Cooper writes, perhaps with Brown in mind, "The American who could write a book — a real, live book — forty years since was a sort of prodigy." The year 1798, in short, dates the appearance, here and in England, of the spirit which there burst forth in the great romantic period that at Scott's death, in 1832, was complete, but which in America had, up to 1832, found no expression in verse more considerable than an enlarged collection of Bryant's early poems. Bryant's opinion of current American poetry in 1818 was that those of his countrymen who read the English poets of the day showed better taste than those who wrote verse. During the first two decades of the century — from Brown's half-dozen novels (once popular in a limited sense, but long ago forgotten) until *The Sketch-Book* and *The Spy* and Bryant's first thin volume of eight poems — the United States were, indeed, a literary desert, with scarcely an oasis save *Knickerbocker's History of New York*, *Thanatopsis*, and *To a Waterfowl*. To say that they then had neither literary past nor present is but to state the arid fact. Fisher Ames went so far at the time as to deny them literary future. Clearly, therefore, *The Sketch-Book* and *The Spy* rank Irving and Cooper as the earliest Americans to make permanent contributions to imaginative prose literature.

The Rev. Jeremy Belknap, founder of the Massachusetts Historical Society, had, it is true, essayed historical fiction in *The Foresters*, which is described as an "allegorical account of the colonial settlements" ; and Isaac Mitchell's *Asylum*, with its castle in Connecticut, and its figure of Franklin dispensing sage counsel to a Yale man, may be mentioned in a necrology or two. But such impotent productions as these, which were never alive, left the field clear for a strong man to nationalise, by putting the American stamp on it, the historical romance which Scott had brought into fashion. So *The Spy*, perhaps begun with a desire to vindicate American independence of British literary precedent, was one of the first proofs that here, too, was romantic material.

The scene was laid in the region which the author knew by living in it, and where traditions of Revolutionary times, when Westchester County had been neutral ground for the armies of invasion and defence, were repeated to him by surviving witnesses of the incidents which they narrated. He used to go among the old farmers, and have them to pass the evening with him, when, over the cider and hickory nuts in the parlor at Angevine, they would tell him about the battle of White Plains and the skirmishes of the Cow-boys, Hessians, and Skinners. In this way he learned all the gossip of the time, and his intercourse with people who had actually taken part with the British enabled him to treat their side fairly. The central character was suggested by a story of John Jay's, who, on retiring from his last public office, the governorship of New York, had gone in 1801 to pass the close of his life on his farm in Westchester. "Then, as he smoked his long clay pipe," says Jay's biographer, "he used to delight in telling anecdotes of the Revolution, the true history of which, he often said, never had been and never would be written." One of these anecdotes, told on a summer afternoon to his son and to Cooper, who had been school-fellows at Albany, was about an agent whom Jay, when chairman of a secret committee appointed by Congress, had employed to gather information of the plans and movements of the British. So deeply had it impressed Cooper that, when he came to write *The Spy* years afterward, the thin, stooping figure of Harvey Birch stepped alive into the scene which was waiting for him. All else in the book is invention.

The first volume, written quickly, was laid aside through fear of failure; and when the tale was taken up after an interval of some months, the publisher, foreseeing that it might run on to an unprofitable length, induced the author to write the last chapter, and to let him print and page it before the plot had been fully contrived — a circumstance for which Cooper afterward apologises without seeking to excuse it. Such haphazard lack of method resulted in a story far less good than might have been made of the material. Cooper was not yet sure of himself. The success, however, was one of the astonishing facts in the history of books. Published anonymously in the autumn of 1821, *The Spy* instantly caught the imagination of America, England, and France. It was dramatised, and translated into almost every European language; and soon Harvey Birch was one of the most popular personages in fiction. Betty Flanagan, too, was warmly commended by so competent a judge of Irish character as Miss Edgeworth. Cooper afterward regretted, with a delicacy of feeling which has gone out of fashion, the introduction into a novel of the revered Washington.

Several pretenders set up claims to identity with the original of Harvey Birch, one man even asserting that "Mr. Cooper used to visit at his house frequently for the purpose of hearing his adventures and writing them out in *The Spy.*" Another claimant was one Enoch Crosby, whose story, as related in a dull volume with no merit save rarity, coincides at several points rather strikingly with that of the patriot peddler.

But the book, to which Cooper himself attached no importance, does not ring true. All such idle tales are scarcely worth recalling. More pertinent, as illustrative of the effect of reality produced by the character, is the anecdote, quoted by Cooper's biographer, that a secret agent of Louis Philippe's prefect of police took Harvey Birch's name, and imitated his conduct.

III.

THE New York of three-quarters of a century ago, though astonishingly in advance of its condition at the opening of the century, cannot now be pictured without a determined effort of imagination, based on study of the amazing growth that has taken place. Suffice it to say that, when Cooper went there to live in 1822, in order to be near his publisher and to put his daughters to school, the house he first rented in Broadway, just above Prince Street, was "almost out of town." The metropolis was then the scene of a good deal of literary activity in a small way, the accounts of which, and of the men who took part in it, are now more entertaining than most of the literary ventures made by the members of the so-called "Knickerbocker School."

In those primitive days the clever men used to meet at the taverns, which served them as clubs, and there discuss everything under the starry cope of heaven. Of course, Cooper founded a club. He called it the Lunch; it is commonly known as the Bread and Cheese. As he made all the nominations, and as one ballot of cheese excluded, the membership was representative and choice; for he knew everybody worth knowing—army and navy officers, lawyers, painters, writers, clergymen, merchants, and men of leisure. Chancellor Kent was a member, and Wiley the publisher, Jarvis the painter and jester, DeKay the naturalist, Durand the engraver and painter, Verplanck the versatile man of letters, Charles King who was afterward president of Columbia, Morse the artist and inventor, Dr. John W. Francis, and the poets Bryant and Halleck. Among men of note who were frequent guests was Bishop Hobart. Cooper and Halleck were the guiding spirits. "Cooper, when in town, was always present," writes Bryant in 1852; "and I remember being struck with the inexhaustible vivacity of his conversation and the minuteness of his knowledge in everything which depended upon acuteness of observation and exactness of recollection." On Thursday evenings these congenial men used to meet at Washington Hall, at the corner of Broadway and Chambers Street, where the Stewart Building now stands. The evening was concluded with a supper, each member taking his turn as caterer, and a coloured woman, Abigail Jones, "carrying out the programme to perfection in the way of cooking."

Meanwhile *The Pioneers* had raised even higher the reputation of the author of *The Spy*. Thirty-five hundred copies are said to have been sold before noon on the day of publication. The scene of the tale is that of Cooper's childhood, and Judge Temple is accepted as a sketch of his father. Some of the incidents are true, and some fictitious. But Natty is as genuine a creation as Rip Van Winkle. "With the exception of his *leathern stockings*, which were worn by a very prosaic old hunter, of the name of Shipman, who brought game to the Hall," there is no foundation in fact for the character who grew in the writer's hands to be the familiar friend of all boys. In this book, in which Natty, "with his silent footfall, stepped from beneath the shadows of the old pines into the winter sunlight," he is less firmly handled and less consistent than in the later *Leather-Stocking* tales, three of which touch on earlier periods of his life. The descriptions, moreover, which charmed the public of 1823 by their spontaneity and native fragrance, make the book seem to us rather dull by comparison with several of those which followed. Had the material been cast in the form of personal reminiscence, it would have been less read then, but would now be more interesting.

An act of kindness deserves to be recorded here. A small volume, entitled *Tales for Fifteen; or, Imagination and Heart*, was published by Wiley in 1823. Some ten or fifteen years afterward Cooper brought home a copy which he had bought, and told his family that he had written the two little stories which it contained, and had given them to his friend Wiley, who was in straits at the time. The paper cover of that now almost unique copy announces as in press the fourth edition of *The Spy*, the third edition of *The Pioneers*, and *The Pilot*.

As all the world may read the introduction in which Cooper tells how *The Pilot* originated in his thinking he could write a more nautical story than Scott's *Pirate*, then new, it will suffice to repeat here that the plot was suggested by Paul Jones's cruise in the *Ranger*, and his descents on Whitehaven and St. Mary's Isle. Each of Cooper's previous books has been surpassed in its kind. *The Pilot* has never been equalled in nautical power, though there are plenty of books about sea life which are better as stories. Oddly enough, Cooper was dissatisfied with Tom Coffin, preferring Boltrope. The superiority of Tom is that his acts are not imaginable as taking place except in the very circumstances in which he, and no one else, performs them; whereas Boltrope talks and conducts himself much as several of Cooper's other old salts might do, and do, in circumstances somewhat similar. Of essentially the same type as Leather-Stocking, Long Tom is not in the slightest degree a copy of him. In fact, the fully developed Leather-Stocking of the later books may rather be said to have some of his predecessor's traits. If it be necessary to look anywhere for the original of the simple-hearted cockswain, perhaps a suggestion may be found in Mr. Irish, the mate of the *Sterling* when Cooper made his voyage before the mast. He, too, was from Nantucket, and was a "prime fellow, and fit to command a ship."

The Pilot was the last of the trio of books which raised their author to a pinnacle of popularity not reached before or since by an American novelist. To the friend to whom he had read passages for criticism before dedicating the tale to him, he wrote from New York, a few weeks after its publication, in topping spirits: "I have been so *stuffed up* with a cold in my head since I got back to good, great, and magnanimous New York, that writing has been altogether out of the question. However, I am obliged to come to the dirty employment once more, and one of my first efforts in that way shall be to let you know how safely I got out of

Yankee-land! I supped at Providence in good season. Next day Newcombe dined with us at Whipple's (being Sunday), and a *good time* we had of it. There was a bottle of old *Blaze-Castle* Madeira, about which there were certain legends of captures in the Revolution and perils by land and perils by water, which I forget; but this I remember well, that after I saw the bulge in the bottom of that bottle, I cared not the snap of a finger for perils of any sort; and the only sense of fear I entertained was, that our host had no more of the precious cordial. . . . The roads were good and the weather tolerable, so I reached home, hearty and hungry. . . .

"*Pilot* is decidedly successful. The sale is the best criterion in such matters, and that is very great. It is very little if any short of *Spy* in popularity, though opinions are as various as men's minds. I found Wiley had the book in the hands of five printers on my return for a reprint. If it has not been as much commended it has certainly been less assailed than any book I have ever written. So much for our *joint* efforts."

Three months later Bryant writes to his wife of meeting Cooper at dinner, where he "engrossed the whole conversation, and seems a little giddy with the great success his works have met with." What wonder that the hearty, cheery, breezy author of *The Spy*, *The Pioneers*, and *The Pilot*—the only American writer of fiction except Irving who had ever had any but a restricted local success—should, by "a certain emphatic frankness" of manner, have "somewhat startled" the shy, retiring country poet who had not yet found his place on the staff of the *Evening Post!* The casual acquaintance thus begun when both were making trial of authorship grew to be an unclouded friendship, based on mutual respect, of which the record remains in the memorial address delivered by Bryant after Cooper's death.

Later in the year 1824, Bryant's friend Richard Henry Dana, poet and essayist, as well as one of the early editors of the *North American Review*, writes from Cambridge of two gentlemen, recently from England, reporting that Cooper was in "high snuff" there, and saying that he "ranks at least with Irving, and that no works meet with a quicker sale." Dana deprecates a knock-kneed article on *The Pilot* by Willard Phillips, which "can do no harm to Cooper," who is "to the windward of the American reviewers, at least." To this Bryant replies: "What you tell me of the success of our countryman, Cooper, in England, is an omen of good things. I hope it is the breaking of a bright day for American literature."

The Pilot was followed by *Lionel Lincoln*, the first of a projected series, never carried further, of "Legends of the Thirteen Republics." Cooper was as careful in preparing it as he had been careless in the case of *The Spy*. "Every effort to preserve accuracy was made. The principal historical authorities, the state papers, official reports, etc., etc., were studied. A journey to Boston was made for the purpose of going over the ground in person. Even almanacs, and records of the weather, were consulted, to insure greater accuracy in detail." Such is Miss Cooper's account of her father's way of setting about a piece of work which he grew tired of and which tires his readers. The method was the reverse of his habit of writing without notes as the mood took him. The natural result was a dull book containing, however, spirited battle-pieces — notably, the battle of Bunker Hill, which is a masterpiece.

Besides the reason just assigned for the failure of the book as a whole, at least one other is worth mentioning. On his return from Boston, Cooper had written "to let you know how safely I got out of Yankee-land!" If ever a New Yorker of Quaker descent, married into a Tory family with a long French lineage, and moving easily among the young "Knickerbocker" group of writers of the early twenties, warmly sympathised with the New Englanders, it was surely not the author of *Lionel Lincoln.* He could, it is true, in the abstract appreciate their manly traits, as is shown by *The Wept of Wish-ton-Wish,* and confirmed by a few lines from a letter dated the year following the publication of that book. "Whatever else I may think of the Yankees," he writes from Paris in 1830, "they are precisely the last people on earth I should attempt to bully out of an opinion. A calmer, firmer, braver people does not walk this earth." But the Puritan character was unattractive to him, and in several subsequent books it suffered grave injustice at his hands. His inability to do the "Yankees" justice has been attributed to similarity in character. He has even been called a "Puritan of the Puritans." He did not, however, so impress his contemporaries; nor do the details of his daily life, as known to us, justify so striking a paradox. It may be met with his own remark that "it takes an aristocrat to make a true democrat"; and that may be supplemented by John Jay's earlier saying that "pure democracy, like pure rum, easily produces intoxication, and with it a thousand mad pranks and fooleries." In short, to sum the matter up in a word, formalism and cant were so odious to Cooper as often to blind him to the good source of which those abuses are the degenerate issue. Like some of the Federalists who made this country, he was a conservative aristocratic republican. The sinews and the unswerving rectitude of the Puritans were his, but no trace of their spiritual exaltation nor of their mystically fervid asceticism.

IV.

WHILE making an excursion with a party of young men to Saratoga and Lake George in 1824, Cooper was urged by Mr. Stanley, afterward Lord Derby, to lay the scene of a story at the curious caverns at Glens Falls. His most brilliant and taking novel, written in three or four months, in the course of which he had a severe attack of fever brought on by exposure to the sun, was the result. Though of course he had read, as a lad, Brockden Brown's *Edgar Huntley*, with its "incidents of Indian hostility and perils of the Western wilderness," yet *The Last of the Mohicans* "would assuredly," as his daughter says, "have been precisely the book it now is, had *Edgar Huntley* never been written." It sprang into instant popularity, which it maintains probably better than any other of its author's books. And no wonder; for its freshness and freedom so win us at fifteen that at fifty we still enjoy meeting again our old friends Hawkeye, Uncas, Chingachgook, and Magua, who are a spirited enough team to draw at a brisk pace the heavy load of the other characters. Though the story, it is true, halts and right-about-faces in the middle, and the horrid slaughter of savages is artistically atrocious, yet, despite more or less fumbling of plot, and a few incidents of sublimated sensationalism, and the error of ending with a lugubrious wail which might better have been a triumphal flourish of trumpets, we readily accept Parkman's testimony to the effect on himself of this and of Cooper's other early books. "The scenes and characters of several of his novels," Parkman writes the year after the publication of his own *Pontiac*, "have been so stamped by the potency of his art upon my mind that I sometimes find it difficult to separate them distinctly from the recollections of my own past experiences. I may say, without exaggeration, that Cooper has had an influence in determining the course of my life and pursuits." This tribute from the close student of Indian life, who by no means approved of Cooper's braves, but held him and Campbell responsible for the bogus warrior that has since become "one of the petty nuisances of literature," is incidentally more pertinent than many a prosy dithyramb on the "noble red man"; for does not the fact that these early stories mingled inseparably with Parkman's recollections of his own experiences go far to establish the reality of Cooper's imaginative sway?

Cooper's Indians, in the dozen books where they appear, neither he nor any one else ever met in the woods. He had read the then duly accredited writers on the subject, had studied delegates from Western tribes who came East, and from childhood had imbibed the

Indian traditions which clung about Otsego Lake and its neighbourhood. Of material thus fortuitously acquired before the present era of scientific study had even dawned he constructed idealised types not more remote from reality than Scott's mediæval knights. As a restoration of a past state of things, *The Last of the Mohicans* bears a certain analogy to *Ivanhoe*. Neither is historically accurate. As literature, however, the one is no more discredited by Bret Harte's travesty than the other is by Thackeray's burlesque. Both have of late been put to the severest test a classic has to undergo: they have been copiously annotated for use as schoolbooks. If they pass unscathed through that unmerited ordeal, then, indeed, may we not call them immortal?

So widely accepted is Cooper's conception of the Indian that to question the truth of the delineation is to disquiet many pious souls by seeming to imply that real Indians are degenerate past redemption. Now, Cooper did present some lofty specimens of manhood in war-paint and feathers, and everybody knows that individual Indians exist as dignified and magnanimous as any of his imagining; but it must be remembered, likewise, that he presented degraded Indians, and that the chief of them all, the subtle Magua, is as incarnate a knave as Iago. Moreover, the best of his Indian tales, being free from polemical or didactic or other extraneous trammel, but written solely because stories of adventure were tingling in his blood, have escaped the imputation of aiming to right the wrongs done the race. Whether ethnological research verify his types, or whether Sims's are better likenesses, matters little. More to the point is the question of the spectacular and dramatic effect of the figures, which any normal boy can answer by saying whether he would have them different.

A letter of Bryant's to Dana at this time (September 1, 1825) gives a glimpse of Cooper: "I saw Cooper yesterday. He is printing a novel entitled *The Last of the Mohicans.* The first volume is nearly finished. You tell me that I must review him next time myself. Ah, sir! he is too sensitive a creature for me to touch. He seems to think his own works his own property, instead of being the property of the public, to whom he has given them; and it is almost as difficult to praise or blame them in the right place as it was to praise or blame Goldsmith properly in the presence of Johnson."

From Broadway the Coopers had moved to Beach Street, and thence to Greenwich Street. In Beach Street the first son, Fenimore, had died; and there Paul, the second son, had been born. The family were looking forward to a trip to Europe, and were diligently studying French and Spanish. In the spring of 1826 Cooper followed to Washington a deputation of Indians, mostly Pawnees and Sioux, in whom he had become interested during their visit to New York. He was studying them with an eye to his next novel, which was begun in New York and finished in Paris. One of these chiefs, described as "a very fine specimen of a warrior, a remarkable man in every way," may have been the model for Hard-Heart, one of the most pleasing of his minor characters. Though not true as a study of a region which the author had never seen, *The Prairie* has qualities which place it high among novels of adventure. Through it runs a strain of poetic feeling for the vague mystery of unlimited expanse, and it has quiet power which grows more impressive on a second or third reading The aged trapper is a nobly pathetic figure, finely contrasted, as Mr. Lounsbury points out, with the squatter. A number of years after the publication of the book, Cooper gives Morse a diverting account of having been pursued from Brussels to Liège by a celebrated animal painter who wanted to make a portrait of him. "His gusto for natural subjects is strong, and his favourite among all my books is 'The Prairie,' which you know is filled with wild beasts. . . . That picture of animal nature had so caught his fancy, that he followed me sixty miles to paint a sketch."

During Cooper's visit to Washington the position of minister to Sweden was offered to him by Clay, the Secretary of State; but he declined it, accepting instead the consulship at Lyons, which he thought would give him greater freedom, and at the same time serve as a protection to his family in the event of European complications. He appears never to have gone there, however; and after a while he gave up the nominal post. On his return to New York his club gave him a farewell dinner, where he said that he meant to write a history of the United States navy, and where Chancellor Kent toasted the "genius which has rendered our native soil classic ground, and given to our early history the enchantment of fiction." When he sailed with his family on board the *Hudson*, on June 1, 1826, for a voyage of five weeks to Cowes, he was apparently ruler of his destiny.

V.

AFTER a delightful week in the Isle of Wight, he went up to London on business with his publisher, leaving his family at Southampton, where he presently rejoined them and crossed to France. Stopping at Rouen, he bought a roomy travelling carriage, in which they made the rest of the journey to Paris. They passed the following year and a half in and about Paris, establishing themselves in the spring of 1827 at St. Ouen, where he wrote *The Red Rover*. As every one may fairly be credited with having read that live book, no remarks on it are needed here beyond a couple of entries, perhaps not universally known, in Scott's *Journal* for January, 1828: "I read Cooper's new novel, *The Red Rover;* the current of it rolls entirely upon the ocean. Something there is too much of nautical language; in fact, it overpowers everything else. . . . He has much genius, a powerful conception of character, and force of execution. The same ideas, I see, recur upon him that haunt other folks. The graceful form of the spars, and the tracery of the ropes and cordage against the sky, is too often dwelt upon." Later in the month he writes: "I have read Cooper's *Prairie*, better, I think, than his *Red Rover*, in which you never get foot on shore, and to understand entirely the incidents of the story it requires too much knowledge of nautical language. It is very clever, though."

The Red Rover was the last novel that added to Cooper's fame until *The Pathfinder* appeared a dozen years later; and much that he wrote and did in the interval diminished his reputation. At this point, therefore, where his position was permanently determined by six of the eight books published in his first and most prosperous period of authorship, a slight indication of his distinctive traits as a writer finds its place.

Detailed discussion of style would here be superfluous; for, as style was the least of Cooper's preoccupations in writing, so it is the last thing one thinks of in reading him. Still, so many gratuitous slurs have been cast on his English, so many well-worn charges have been brought, which to particularise were trite and tedious, that it becomes necessary to insist rather on the virtues which equally exist in his writing. All that is needful for clearness may be briefly stated. His style is said to be, in general, commonplace, careless, and prolix, frequently lumbering and involved. Especially in scenes of what is conventionally termed polite society it doubtless misses the mark. The narrative, moreover, sometimes lags so that the listless reader is disposed to get behind and push. But when the story is fairly going, on the waves or in the woods, the style for the time rises to the occasion, and often for a stretch of fifty pages or more is suitable, adequate, unpretentious, and free from mannerism. Whoever questions its efficiency for its purpose may open *The Last of the Mohicans* at the description of the falls, or may read again the account of the battle of Bunker Hill in *Lionel Lincoln*, or the adventures of the sleighing party in *Satanstoe*, or the famous fifth chapter of *The Pilot*. That chapter, the first in fiction to show that the master of the sea tale had come into the world, is unsurpassed in the literature of the sea. Its effect, acknowledged by all the critics who mention it, has been felt by every one of the million boys whom it has enthralled in the last three-quarters of a century. The man who wrote it made alive as never before the ship and the element with which she battled, and in some degree gave semblance of life to those aboard her. How, unless by instinctively right choice and arrangement of words?

Cooper's supreme power in depicting the brooding of the weather is perfectly shown by a short passage in a later chapter of *The Pilot*, where, in reply to Tom's prediction of a storm, Barnstable says: "'Your prophecy is idle, this time, Master Coffin; everything looks like a dead calm. This swell is what is left from the last blow; the mist overhead is nothing but the nightly fog, and you can see, with your own eyes, that it is driving seaward; even this land-breeze is nothing but the air of the ground mixing with that of the ocean; it is heavy with dew and fog, but it's as sluggish as a Dutch galliot.'

"'Ay, sir, it is damp, and there is little of it,' rejoined Tom; 'but as it comes only from the shore, so it never goes far on the water. It is hard to learn the true signs of the weather,

Captain Barnstable, and none get to know them well, but such as study little else, or feel but little else. There is only One who can see the winds of heaven, or who can tell when a hurricane is to begin, or where it will end. Still, a man isn't like a whale or a porpoise, that takes the air in his nostrils, but never knows whether it is a south-easter or a north-wester that he feeds upon. Look, broad-off to leeward, sir; see the streak of clear sky shining under the mists; take an old sea-faring man's word for it, Captain Barnstable, that whenever the light shines out of the heavens in that fashion, 'tis never done for nothing; besides, the sun set in a dark bank of clouds, and the little moon we had was dry and windy.' "

The quality of this English may be tested by comparison with Defauconpret's translation into French, which, though not far wrong as a translation, somehow manages to destroy the savour of the salt. In the characteristically direct, simple, idiomatic original every word tells, and helps to produce the vague foreboding which is justified by the wreck of the *Ariel.* The passage is as difficult to phrase differently as one of Stevenson's nicely adjusted paragraphs. Were all Cooper's pages equal to that, he would be called a master of English.

In description of nature, afloat and ashore, the good qualities of his style almost invariably predominate. His volumes of travel are so picturesque and entertaining as to lead a discriminating critic to pronounce them "among the best of their kind." His familiar letters of friendship or affection have colloquial ease and graphic lightness. The words of a few of his characters — Harvey Birch, Tom Coffin, Leather-Stocking — are life-like. In short, where he feels at home with his subject, the style responds without apparent effort to a natural impulse. On the other hand, when he tries to produce an effect with thankless or uncongenial material, the style is inert; for he wrote precipitately, and spurned revision.

The gist of the matter is that Cooper was not a verbal artist, and that his endowment of what we are pleased to call literary conscience was scant. With no special training as a writer, when, at thirty or thereabout, it accidentally came into his head to try his hand at a novel, he struck boldly out, not particularly considering whither. Some of his early books, written for his own pleasure, brought him popularity which surprised no one more than himself. The art of writing engaged his attention far less than the panorama and the story. Robust and impetuous, he disdained details of style and academic standards. To apply to him academic standards is as if one should inquire whether Hard-Heart's horsemanship conforms to the rules of the riding-school; for nobody cares. It is to miss the point that, heaven knows how or why, he struck — Heaven be praised! — a new trail which, admitting all the shortcomings in style that any one may choose to allege, the world is not yet weary of following. The indisputable, the essential fact is that, entering unheralded and possessing the land, he founded a realm, and became by divine right king of American fiction. Scott, with whom he is often idly, though perhaps inevitably, compared, had behind him generations of literary association in a country which teemed with thronging suggestion of romance, and which was peopled by an eager audience. The American writers of that early time were, as Bayard Taylor said, "even in advance of their welcome, and created their own audiences." To no such heritage as Scott's was Cooper born. Alone he penetrated and permeated the literary wilderness, blazing paths for those who should come after. To disparage his work on the score of lack of technical finish is to subordinate primary considerations to secondary, and to prove one's self dull to that rarest of endowments, that precious literary prize—originality.

It was during Cooper's first residence in Paris, in 1826, that Scott called on him. Cooper's detailed account of their meetings, and of his efforts to secure for Scott pecuniary compensation in this country, is generally known; and Scott mentions the subject in his *Journal.* Scott's only recorded personal impression of Cooper is in these words: "This man, who has shown so much genius, has a good deal of the manner, or want of manner, peculiar to his countrymen." An unlucky misprint in Lockhart's *Life of Scott* made this innocent remark offensive by the accidental addition of an *s* to the word *manner.* When Cooper came to review Lockhart's work for the *Knickerbocker Magazine* in 1838, he properly resented being thus curtly set down as a rude boor from the bookless wilds. The slur cast on himself and his country by the man whom he had spoken of as his "sovereign," with whom his relations had been cordial, and in whose behalf he had been fruitlessly zealous, unquestionably sharpened the edge of some criticisms in that review for which he was violently assailed in England. Not until the publication of the *Journal* in its authentic form, many years too late to repair the damage done, was Scott's sentence printed as he wrote it.

During the four months that Cooper passed in London, in 1828, he saw many of the interesting persons of the day, of whom he tells sundry entertaining anecdotes. He took a small house in St. James's Place. Rogers, his near neighbour, was among the first to call on him, and had him frequently to breakfast, where he met Lord John Russell, Sir James Mackintosh, and Carey, the translator of Dante. He says of Rogers, whom he liked, that "few men have a more pleasant way of saying pleasant things"; and he calls Sir James "the best talker I ever heard," and "the only man I have yet met in England who appears to have any clear and definite notions of us." He was soon dining at Holland House, and meeting the leading Whigs, of whom Lord Grey seemed to him "the man of the most character in his set, though he betrayed it quietly, naturally, and, as it were, as if he could not help it." He saw something of Coleridge, "a picture of green old age,—ruddy, solid, and with a head as white as snow." Scott, whom he met several times, he speaks of on one occasion as having "a good stately chat with Mrs. Siddons, who *dialogued* with him in a very Shaksperian manner." Enough has been quoted from the book on England, published four years after his return to America, to show that he was a keen casual observer. He was also a minute critic of social and national traits, and an aggressive patriot, stirred to emphatic utterance by disparagement of his country. He accordingly wrote *Notions of the Americans; Picked up by a Travelling Bachelor*, a somewhat ponderous defence of American institutions against the attacks on them then prevalent in Europe. Though calm in tone and acute in dealing with facts of which he had wide and accurate knowledge, the book, meant to enlighten and to clear away misapprehension, had the effect of drawing on its author a fire of criticism both at home and abroad. Its publication, in the same year with *The Red Rover*, marks the beginning of the wave of personal unpopularity which subsequently swept over him.

Though especially well treated in England, he found himself ill at ease with the people, and was glad to escape in June to more congenial countries. First he went to Holland, and, passing through Belgium, returned to Paris. Thence he went to Switzerland, where he hired a house near Berne. Crossing the Simplon in October, he passed nine months in Tuscany. "In July, 1829, the whole family," he writes, "went to Leghorn, where I chartered a felucca and sailed for Naples, touching at Elba, Piombino, Civita Vecchia, and one or two of the small islands. We were six days on board, and were somewhat bitten by fleas. Oh Napoli! glorious, sunny, balmy Napoli! We staid five months at Naples, or near it, and in December went up to Rome." Leaving Rome in April, he passed a month at Venice, and in June went, by way of the Tyrol, to Dresden. "Here we staid," he writes in September, 1830, "until the Revolution broke out in Paris, when I came on post, and Mrs. Cooper followed with the children at her leisure. We are now fixed for six months. It is my present intention to return home in about a year, though political events may induce me to alter my plans." Delight in the scenery of Switzerland, and especially in the refinement of natural beauty in Italy, pervades the *Sketches of Switzerland* and *Gleanings in Europe*, which tell in detail the experiences of the two years of travel. Incidentally containing much tart criticism of things American which enraged some of his sensitive countrymen, those books are largely a record, in the form of letters to friends at home, of his fresh impressions of what he saw. Of the witchery of Italy, the land he loved next to his own, he speaks with contagious joy and stimulating intelligence. With the possible exception of a few scenes at sea, some of the Italian descriptions are as spontaneously vital as anything that he wrote.

At La Lorraine, his country-house

near Berne, from which he used to watch the glaciers of the Oberland Alps in the setting sun, *The Wept of Wish-ton-Wish* was begun; but owing to difficulties in getting a printer, it was not published until he had been for some time in Florence. That was followed by *The Water Witch*, which was partly written at the Casa Tasso, on the cliffs of Sorrento, was condemned by the censor at Rome because it contained the words, "Rome itself is only to be traced by fallen temples and buried columns," and was eventually published in Dresden. Next came *The Bravo*, "written to martial music" in Paris, in 1830, and followed by *The Heidenmauer* and *The Headsman*. These three "novels with a purpose," seeking to teach the world the superiority of a popular government to an oligarchy, naturally incurred (as didactic fiction has a way of doing) criticism based rather on the merits of the doctrine inculcated than on their own. Again and again Cooper failed when he essayed to tell his readers what he thought they ought to be told, and succeeded when he had in view only the story which fired his own imagination. As has often been said in one form or another, his early novels taught Europe more about America than Europe had ever before learned, whereas his dissertations on American matters were apt to lead only to befogging controversy. *The Bravo*, which was far better received in France and Germany than at home, has, it is true, considerable merit; so has *The Headsman;* but neither has the special qualities which set some half-dozen of his novels in a class apart, unmatched.

In whatever country Cooper happened to be, he sedulously studied current events; and sometimes he made shrewd political forecasts — as, for instance, of the unification of Italy, which as early as 1829 he thought "inevitable, though the means by which it is to be effected are still hidden." The turmoil in Paris had, accordingly, attracted him at once to the scene of action, where he might have a near view of the Revolution of July. For a while he lived in the rue d'Aguesseau, and then across the river at 59 rue St. Dominique until his return to America.

Several features of Cooper's second residence in Paris were wholly satisfactory. Lafayette, whom he had known in New York in 1824, when he was active in getting up the famous ball at Castle Garden in honour of the "nation's guest," he esteemed as a friend of liberty and of America. In Paris, where Lafayette was now the centre of the American circle, he saw him constantly and intimately. That true American, Horatio Greenough, who had basked in the hospitable warmth of Cooper's wood fires in Florence, after a while came to Paris to make a bust of Lafayette. Well might Greenough call Cooper "a father to me in kindness"; for it was Cooper's order for the marble group of the Chanting Cherubs, the "first work of the kind," as Cooper wrote from Dresden, "which has come from an American chisel," that eventually led to Greenough's making the statue of Washington. Samuel Gridley Howe, already active in good works, whom Sydney Smith, on hearing the story of Laura Bridgman, likened to Pygmalion, was in Paris for a time, studying medicine. In 1832 Nathaniel Parker Willis was making pencil sketches of the ravening cholera, breakfasting with Cooper, and strolling with him in the Garden of the Tuileries. Morse was painting at the Louvre, helping Cooper in the choice of pictures to buy, taking long afternoon walks with him, and a little later hinting to him the possibility of stringing the telegraphic wire. "We were in daily, almost hourly, intercourse," writes Morse some twenty years afterward, "while in Paris during the eventful years of 1831, 1832. I never met with a more sincere, warm-hearted, constant friend. No man came nearer to the ideal I had formed of a truly high-minded man.'' Their relations were, in fact, peculiarly warm and close. Another man of note, between whom and Cooper had sprung up an attachment as they scoured the Roman Campagna together, was Mickiewicz, the Polish poet and patriot, the insurrection of whose countrymen, following soon after the Revolution in France, enlisted the impassioned interest of the American champion of freedom. As an active member of the American committee for the relief of the suffering Poles, Cooper by public speaking and by writing zealously aided the cause of the insurgents.

On all questions involving natural rights, his heart and his head concurred. In 1830 he writes to a friend at home about nullification: ''The present state of feeling in South Carolina is well known to me, and has given me much pain. From very early life, I have had much intercourse with gentlemen of your state, and I have always felt an attachment for its people. But it is impossible to avoid seeing that an evil spirit is at work among them just now." An extremely minute examination of the whole matter follows, concluding in this masculine language: "These truths are so clear and imposing, that I am tempted to think they [the nullifiers] are only bullying, which is both an ill-advised and an unworthy attempt. Indeed, the whole proceedings in Carolina, beyond that part which has certainly a good deal of foundation in right, are too much characterised by passion to carry any confidence to men of cool heads. They flatter themselves they are imitating their fathers, but nothing can be more unlike. Their fathers were cool and dignified and conciliatory, but these Hotspurs begin with talking about 'leaden pills,' and by using other bravadoes. I believe all freemen are brave, but when a handful of them use this sort of language to millions, they give some reason to distrust their possessing that very thought which is the foundation of all durable courage. To conclude, I think they are acting in the very worst taste, and in the very worst policy, too, in a cause that is more than half right. . . . Knowing your own moderation, I am persuaded you will agree with me that bad taste, as well as indiscretion, has had too much influence of late over some men that we both esteem, for their ordinary habits and principles. I commit them to the Gods."

Regard for Lafayette drew Cooper, in 1831, into what is known as the "Expenses' Controversy," which it is necessary to mention, not for its own sake, but because its results affected his life. As briefly as possible, the bare facts, condensed from Lounsbury, are these. A financial discussion in the Chamber of Deputies had brought from the editor of the *Revue Britannique* an article to prove that a limited monarchy costs less than a republic. It was pointed out to Cooper that this was an attack on his friend Lafayette, who held the government of the United States to be the cheapest known. He accordingly published a pamphlet which the *Revue Britannique* answered in an article to which he replied in letters to the *National*. Further controversy ensued, in which Cooper's opponent was an American, whose statements gained factitious authoritativeness with foreigners from his having once been *chargé d'affaires* at St. Petersburg, and his being afterward appointed to the same post at Paris. Meanwhile the Department of State at Washington had issued a circular requesting of local authorities information regarding public expenditure. In a letter written at Vevey in the autumn of 1832, published in the Philadelphia *National Gazette*, and widely circulated, Cooper protested so stoutly against such a confusion of the subject that the matter dropped. Notoriety, however, attached to him for his part in the contest. As usual, he was misrepresented by a portion of the press, and was charged by certain vociferous persons with "flouting his Americanism throughout Europe," and with committing various other indiscretions.

Had he carried out his original plan of returning home in 1831, he would have been spared the disenchantment and discouragement resulting from this unfortunate episode. During his second visit to Switzerland he had written: "A few toad-eaters and court butterflies excepted, I do not believe there is a man in all America who could dwell five years in any country in Europe, without being made sensible of the vast superiority of his own free institutions over those of every other Christian nation." That feeling never changed. Yet the lack of appreciation of it so turned awry his generous impulses that when he finally left Europe after an absence of almost seven years and a half, he had firmly resolved to lay down the pen.

VI.

THE next few winters he passed in New York, and the summers at beautiful Cooperstown. Otsego Hall was renovated according to designs made by Morse, and became eventually his permanent residence. "The Hall," he writes in 1835, "is composite enough, Heaven knows, being a mongrel of the Grecian and the Gothic orders. Who has told you anything about it? It is a good substantial house, and, on the whole, I think a good-looking house, though there are striking defects. It is not an easy matter to 'raise upon' a house, or a ship, and preserve its good looks. My hall, however, is the admiration of all the mountaineers. It is near fifty feet long, twenty-four wide, and fifteen high. These are no marvels for your traveller, but for the interior of New York they are. The only change in it, since my boyhood, however, is in the height. I have raised the ceiling three feet, and now regret it had not been ten. I have an aversion to a room under jury masts." There he kept open house to his friends, cultivated his garden, grew melons and vegetables, planted hemlocks, and assiduously gathered material for the forthcoming history of the navy. He also, to his sorrow, became involved in a series of litigations which can here be only outlined. The subject can be fully understood only through laborious ransacking of files of newspapers long ago dead and dusty. A few pages, however, will suffice to show how it all began, and what came of it, and — more important still — how he bore himself in the tempest which he unloosed and finally quelled. Throughout the ensuing trouble his acts must be looked at, if not from his point of view, at least in the light of his character.

"I see Cooper occasionally in his visits

to town, for he lives in the country. He is a restless creature, and does not seem well satisfied with his position in this country, though his great reputation, his handsome fortune, his fine health, and his very amiable family ought to make him so." Bryant, writing thus to Dana at the end of February, 1837, was probably not fully cognisant of all that had taken place in Cooper's life during the three or four years preceding, and was certainly not in his confidence regarding all his thoughts and feelings.

As a matter of fact, Cooper had stayed abroad too long, and had come home to a country that he did not know and that did not know him ; for both had changed in the interval. He had left the stage-coach, and had returned to the railway ; he had left in the White House John Quincy Adams, the last President who inherited Federalist traditions, and had found him succeeded by Jackson ; he had left a society in which the aristocratic ideal had not lost its prestige, and had come back to see a younger generation, regardless of the past, pressing tumultuously in every direction for new opportunities and new outlets for its energy, and apparently striving toward no definite goal except the dollar. With this young America he was not in sympathy; for his tastes had been developed by civilisations which were mature before ours was dreamed of, and his heart turned fondly to the past. He had an Horatian hatred of the mediocrity which is a foe to excellence, and which then obscured that future which has become the past we are so proud of. Not that he was not always proud of his country: no one ever loved it more dearly. For that very reason he deprecated the degeneracy resulting from the commercial spirit of the day, and he unwisely took it on himself to lecture his countrymen on their shortcomings. We have always been absurdly sensitive about that sort of thing, morbidly eager to hear what any stray tourist may have to say of us, and ready to bridle up at the slightest uncomplimentary suggestion. It is a national trait. Mr. Archer calls it "a psychological necessity, deep rooted in history and social conditions." Be that as it may, Miss Martineau, Mrs. Trollope, Marryat, and Dickens (to mention only conspicuous names) all angered us by their comments, and are not yet forgiven. But they were British, and our natural enemies. Cooper's crime was treason. For had he not attacked the abuses of that "precious pest and necessary mischief," the "prostituted companion of liberty, and somehow or other, we know not how, its efficient auxiliary," as Fisher Ames calls the press? "Each hour, as life advances," Cooper had written in the introduction to *The Heidenmauer*, "am I made to see how capricious and vulgar is the immortality conferred by a newspaper."

What wonder that the retort should have been, "The press has built him up: the press shall pull him down"! American scenery, too, he belittled, and bewailed the departure of old-fashioned simplicity from American manners. The indiscriminate laudation of everything American drove him to vivacity of expression about whatever impressed him as crude or ungenuine. "If it be patriotism to deem all our geese swans," he wrote, "I am no patriot, nor ever was; for, of all species of sentiments, it strikes me that your 'property patriotism' is the most equivocal." In the thirties, when untravelled and inexperienced America scarcely understood the meaning of the accounts of European countries brought back by the few Americans who went abroad, that was rank heresy. Moreover, popular taste in fiction had veered. The romantic wave had begun to subside even before Scott's death, and heroes of the Pelham stripe had come into fashion. Thus several causes worked together to place Cooper, both as a man and as an author, in a false position; and he cannot be said to have done his utmost to counteract them. There is pertinence in Horatio Greenough's picturesque remark that he "lost hold on the American public by rubbing down their shins with brickbats."

It is not true, however, that he strutted about with a chip on his shoulder, picking a quarrel with whoever crossed his path. He had said in Paris, in 1832, on the appearance of an acrimonious article in an American newspaper: "I care nothing for the criticism, but I am not indifferent to the slander. If these attacks on my character should be kept up five years after my return to America, I shall resort to the New York courts for protection." For five years thereafter he acted with moderation under a rising storm of calumny. When, in 1837, it passed endurance, he joined battle, careless of consequences, with all comers, and fought till he had cleared the field. Galling though his words often were, he did not strike the first blow.

In *A Letter to His Countrymen*, published in 1834, Cooper injudiciously answered certain newspaper criticisms on *The Bravo* and the later novels, and still more injudiciously discussed the political situation — subjects with nothing in common. Caleb Cushing replied like an irate gentleman to the political part of the pamphlet; but the Whig press sprang, with what Cooper's biographer calls a "howl of denunciation," at the pamphleteer. *The Monikins*, an unreadable satirical novel, was published the next year; and in the three years following came ten volumes of travel in Switzerland, France, England, and Italy, entertaining in parts, but irritating to their first readers on account of the comments on social and national idiosyncrasies. The book on England seems to have been the one by which its author set most store. "Have you read England—and if so how do you like it?" he writes in the autumn of 1837. "They tell me it has made a stir in London, where I get abused and read *à la* Trollope. . . . It ought to do them good, but whether it will or not depends on Divine grace." And later in the same year, four or five months after Emerson's Φ. B. K. oration which Holmes called "our intellectual Declaration of Independence," he continues: "I am glad you like England, for I think books of this spirit much wanted. I am afraid, however, it is not very well received in general. It is in advance of the country. . . . We must make up our minds, I fear, to live our time as the inhabitants of a mere colony. A century hence things will improve, perhaps, but not in our day." But *England*, which appeared in the year of Queen Victoria's accession, could never have been a timely publication; for, clever and penetrating and true as parts of it are, the book as a whole lacks amenity, without which criticism can do little good. It is certainly not a production in which either nation can rejoice and be glad, but is rather calculated to set people by the ears than to save them from their sins. Its effect on the *Quarterly Review* was to make it foam at the mouth in stupid rage. To the Swiss and Italian volumes justice could be done only by profuse quotation. Such an amalgam of excellent description and caustic animadversion it is not easy to match. The description, which may still be read with unmixed pleasure, made no impression; the censure, which now is rather diverting, was thought pragmatical, acrid, and insolent.

These books went far to strengthen the hostility to Cooper, which had meanwhile been precipitated by the Three

Mile Point controversy between him and a gang of his fellow-townsmen. On his return to Cooperstown he had found that the villagers regarded as public property a point of land, called Myrtle Grove, which Judge Cooper had bequeathed to his descendants until 1850, "then to be inherited by the youngest thereof bearing my name." Though willing to let the people use the place for picnics, as they had long been accustomed to do, he was determined, as the last of his father's executors, to "enforce the title of the estate." He published a card to that effect, warning the public against trespassing. A meeting was thereupon called, at which it was resolved to hold his threat and his whole conduct "in perfect contempt"; to have his books removed from the village library; and to "denounce any man as sycophant, who has, or shall, ask permission of James F. Cooper to visit the Point in question." There was even a report that it had been resolved to make a public bonfire of all his works. Cooper had these resolutions printed; and he wrote to the *Freeman's Journal*, the local Democratic newspaper, two defiant letters, giving the whole history of the case, and stoutly defending the village against the charge that the rowdy meeting was representative.

This took place in the summer of 1837. In September, Cooper thus refers to the next step in the proceedings: "The Point war is over, I believe, all but the libel suits. I got the resolutions and published them myself, with a few comments, and this has mortified them not a little. But the disgrace of our democrats trembling to say what they think of their conduct, will last a long time in my mind.

"Some of the neighbouring newspapers have attacked the villagers, and the Otsego Republican makes feeble and insignificant answers, but the editor is too great an ass to notice. He has never dared to answer me, although he talks very prettily of my 'unqualified hostility!' the blackguard, after grossly libelling me. My letter made them look blue, and I believe the greater part would be glad to forget the whole affair. One of the few decent men who were at the meeting admitted to me that its statements were false, its proceedings illegal, indecent and outrageous. In truth, a grosser outrage could not well have been practised."

In writing later to an officer who had recently been in command of the West India squadron, one who likewise received his share of detraction from men of coarser fibre, Cooper thus casually refers to an element in the matter which constantly affected his own relations with his adversaries: "Do you know that you have been had up before a meeting of gentlemen (gamblers) at Pensacola, and denounced? This is *your*

Three Mile Point affair. The sin was refusing to associate with blackguards, I suppose, which is my great offence, here. In this part of the world it is thought aristocratic not to frequent taverns, and lounge at corners, squirting tobacco juice, and I dare say it is no better at Pensacola. One scamp is surprisingly like another all over the world." Cooper, it is clear, in all his libel suits stood for a social class. But, besides the antipathy which he inspired on that account, the political differences between him and his adversaries, hinted at in the first of the letters just quoted, are not to be overlooked. Though a protectionist, he was a Democrat, whereas the defendants in the suits were Whig editors. As the Democratic editors kept almost unbroken silence, the outcry of the populace, uttered through the accredited organs of a political party, was to be braved by one man.

This skirmish at Cooperstown led at

once to a pitched battle. The first suit for libel was brought against the editor of the Otsego *Republican*, above mentioned, for an article described by Horace Greeley as "urging that their [the villagers'] extrusion from 'The Point,' though legal, was churlish, and impelled by the spirit of the dog in the manger." Cooper states the fact in a letter dated October 2, 1837: "I hear the enemy is a good deal ashamed of himself, which is showing more grace than I thought he possessed. Symptoms of giving in on the part of our editor, who must succumb completely, or 'abide the time,'—for I have sued him. His Mæcenas told me yesterday, he had advised him to come to me and say that he was willing to let me publish any statement I pleased to correct his own mistakes he had made himself. To which I answered this would not do. He had published falsehoods as from *himself*, and he must correct them as from *himself*, or take the consequences."

Homeward Bound and its sequel, *Home as Found*, written in hot haste, were published the next year. The adventures at sea and the battle with Arabs have earned for the first some civil remarks; but nothing has ever been said in extenuation of *Home as Found*, which was a monumental and calamitous blunder. Its pictures of the press and of New York society infuriated New Yorkers, and drew from the newspapers such execration as makes one blush for one's countrymen. The ferocity of the American press was, if possible, surpassed by the disingenuousness and brutality of *Blackwood* and *Fraser*, the *Quarterly*, and even the *Times*, all of which in their assaults on Cooper for his *England* and his review of Lockhart's *Life of Scott* sullied their pages with rancorous contumely.

Goaded by the turbulent mob, Cooper closed with his traducers. Whoever denies him vocabulary cannot have read his controversial writings. His invective was a weapon of far more exquisite temper than that of the rioters; for, whereas they descended to arraignment of motives and to defamation of character, his most flaming anger never made him forget that the ruffianly conduct of others need not interfere with his remaining a gentleman. His annihilating retorts, being neither falsehoods nor personal insults, were not actionable.

The year after the Point controversy Cooper published *The American Democrat*, incidentally excoriating the press. The next year he recovered a verdict against the Cooperstown editor whom he had sued in 1837. The Chenango *Telegraph* and the Oneida *Whig*, small local sheets, were also prosecuted, as likewise Park Benjamin's *Evening Signal* of New York. In May, 1839, appeared *The History of the Navy of the United States of America*. A year later Horace Greeley, editor of the *New Yorker*, jauntily writes: "Mr. Cooper proved not long ago that the editor of the *Chenango Telegraph* had taken away his character, and a liberal jury awarded him four hundred dollars in payment for it. He has obtained several characters, it seems, since then, and they have all been stolen away; for he is suing, to recover their value, the supposed robbers. He has sued Col. Stone of the *Commercial* for proving that his Naval History is a shallow book, and on Wednesday of this week he instituted proceedings against Park Benjamin for depriving him of his 'reputation.' If Benjamin is guilty, we are at a loss to know what he wanted to do with such a worthless commodity, unless he intends to bestow it on some of his enemies." According to Benjamin, that would seem to have been the best disposition to make of it; for he had said that blackguarding was "as natural to Cooper as snarling to a tom-cat or growling to a bull-dog," and had called him the "common mark of scorn and contempt of every well-informed American," and a "superlative dolt." Throughout these years such envenomed stuff tainted newspapers, big and little, in all parts of the country, one copying another's remarks, and re-enforcing them with commendatory comments. It was doubtless thought good sport to irritate a man who the editors did not at first suppose could harm them. Moreover, the scandal of course served the important end of circulating the newspapers.

Cooper held other views of the function of the press. A letter which he sent to the *Journal of Commerce* in 1840, but which appears not to have been printed, describes a libel as "injurious, false, and malicious," points out a newspaper's power for good and for bad, and states his own position. The pretension of the press to be the voice of the people he denies. The press is, on the contrary, a mere aggregate of independent sheets, each existing primarily to make money, and each giving voice to the opinions of its editor, who is, therefore, as strictly accountable as any other man for personal attacks. An author's right of criticism and an editor's are mutual. Each may handle the other's published work as roughly as he pleases, but neither may touch on the other's private affairs. For the abuse of these rights the press seeks a pretext in its own alleged impersonality, leaving to the author whose character is assailed no resort but the law. To be worthy of their high calling, editors must come to understand their personal responsibility, and not infringe the rights of others. With more to like purpose, Cooper supports the unpopular cause, making it clear that he understands the law of libel, as well as the pettiness of a large part of the press.

Truly, the American press of 1840

was provincial. How could it be otherwise, when steam was in leading-strings and electricity had not learned the alphabet; when the journey from Albany to New York took all day, and an answer to a letter to England did not come for at least a month; when the Albany *Evening Journal* — a badly printed four-page sheet, ten years old — was three parts advertisements, and the *Tribune* did not exist? Newspapers now have their full stint of faults; but they do give a true history of the world, together with the opinions of all kinds of people from every quarter of the globe. The better sort no longer depend for circulation wholly on local happenings and on scandal. As the field has widened, provinciality has been to a great extent replaced by breadth of view.

Seeing what the press was and perhaps dreaming of what it might be, Cooper, when attacked by a creature he despised, took steps to protect himself.

The opposition gathered force. He stood alone. Assisted only by his nephew, Richard Cooper, he dexterously conducted to a successful issue suits against the most powerful newspapers in the country, defended by the ablest counsel.

James Watson Webb, editor of the New York *Courier and Inquirer*, who had lived at Cooperstown as a youth, was criminally indicted in 1839 for a marvellous rigmarole purporting to be a review of *Home as Found*. In the course of an endless farrago of fact and invention, Cooper is styled a "base-minded caitiff who has traduced his country for filthy lucre and low-born spleen," and a "slanderer who is in fact a traitor to national pride and national character." Webb's remarks on the first indictment led to a second, which was dismissed on his retraction of the statement that the first had been "secured by political trickery." The case, which was tried twice, and during which *Home as Found* was read as evidence, was finally dismissed in 1843 on account of the second disagreement of the jury. "Satisfied with this experience," writes Thurlow Weed, "Mr. Cooper procured no more indictments, but thenceforward preferred the civil to the criminal side of the calendar."

Thurlow Weed, of ingratiating manner and velvety voice, who when a lad served his apprenticeship as journeyman printer at Cooperstown, and in time became, in partnership with Seward and Greeley, one of the consummate politicians of America, was then the astute editor of the Albany *Evening Journal*, the acknowledged leader of the Whig press. Immediately after the affair of the Three Mile Point he had copied into the *Journal* the article from the Otsego *Republican*, "supplementing it," he says, "with some approving remarks." Weed was not sued, however, until 1840; and the case did not come to trial at Fonda until October, 1841. As the defendant did not appear, judgment went by default. Weed thereupon wrote to the *Tribune*, then six months old, his version of the case. Horace Greeley published the letter, and was promptly sued. Weed, disconcerted at his failure in a matter which he had at first not taken seriously, resorted to the device of collecting paragraphs from newspapers in the State of New York and elsewhere, and printing them, a column or more at a time, under the heading, COOPERAGE — a caption lending itself readily to weak verbal quibbles which made mirth for the groundlings. He also contributed, as occasion served, editorial articles on the subject, some of them virulent. One of his reprints, referring to Cooper's refusal to believe that Weed's non-appearance in court was due to illness in his family, contains the words: "He might as well have appealed to the reddest of the great novelist's Indians when the war-paint was on him, and the scalps of the palefaces hung reeking at his belt." The republication of this article, and of others, was construed as libellous, Weed's testimony to matters of fact was excluded as irrelevant, and the jury, under the judge's instruction, found for the plaintiff. Suit followed suit, the press asserting its liberty to attack the individual, and Cooper denying its right to invade private life. The fight on both sides was relentless. As Weed was invariably defeated, he at length decided that his better policy was to "withdraw the injurious imputations . . . on the character of Mr. Cooper" which he had been making. This unrepentant retraction, "as broad as the charges," he published, with a bad grace, in the *Journal* of December 14, 1842.

Horace Greeley's case came on at

Ballston in that month. He appeared in answer to the summons, admitted his publication of Weed's letter, and "accepted the responsibility thereof." Richard Cooper opened for the plaintiff, Greeley replied, and Fenimore Cooper summed up "in a longer and rather stronger speech than Richard's." The judge then "bullied the jury" into finding for the plaintiff. So says Greeley. Hastening back to New York, he narrated his experience in an interminable article for the next morning's *Tribune*, which many people found highly enlivening, and for which he was at once sued. This time he was defended by Seward, who spoke of "vindictive damages" and of "star chamber rescripts of libel," and succeeded in staving off a final trial.

Thus Cooper, conscientiously fighting for principle, after some six years discomfited, without reforming, the press, which still hurled adjectives at his head. He gained, as was said, "the reputation of a proud, captious, censorious, arbitrary, dogmatical, malicious, illiberal, revengeful, and litigious man"; or, as Greeley, anticipating Whistler, more neatly turns it, of one "combining in his manners what a Yankee once characterized as 'winning ways to make people hate him.'" The unpopularity, as such, did not seriously distress a man so rich in resources as Cooper, but, naturally, it saddened and somewhat embittered him; for "What deep wounds ever closed without a scar?" It so curtailed the sale of his novels that some people who had read the early ones as boys were scarcely aware of the existence of any subsequent to *The Red Rover*, and that he was led to say in 1843: "I know that many of the New York booksellers are afraid to touch my works, on account of the press of that righteous and enlightened emporium."

The feeling of those who knew him

best — a strain of men whom it is instructive to compare with some who spoke ill of him — is expressed by his friend Morse, who had his own experience of litigation. "It is not because I have not thought of you and your excellent family," he wrote from New York while the rage of the multitude was maddest, "that I have not long since written you, to know your personal welfare. I hear of you often, it is true, through the papers. They praise you as usual, for it is praise to have the abuse of such as abuse you. In all your libel suits against these degraded wretches, I sympathise entirely with you, and there are thousands who now thank you in their hearts for the moral courage you display in bringing these licentious scamps to a knowledge of their duty. Be assured the good sense, the intelligence, the right feeling of the community at large are with you. The licentiousness of the press needed the rebuke which you have given it; and it feels it, too, despite its awkward attempts to brave it out. I will say nothing of your *Home as Found.* I will use the frankness to say that I wish you had not written it. But when am I ever to see you? Do call on me if you come to the city."

In 1850 the Point went, by the terms of Judge Cooper's will, to his namesake, William Cooper. He leased it as a picnicking ground to the village, which purchased it of him in 1899. Thus after sixty-two years the incident was closed.

VII.

In May, 1839, when Cooper was almost fifty, appeared the *Naval History*, which he had been pondering for some fifteen years, and pretty steadily preparing ever since his return from Europe in 1833. His information, especially about the War of 1812, he got largely from officers who were engaged; and he spared no pains to insure accuracy by examination of official records. With unusual knowledge of ships and of maritime affairs, and with special power of presenting such subjects, he produced a classic which, though now unread, has value of a sort that can belong to no subsequent treatment of the period covered. There are officers in the navy who remember their delight on first reading those accounts of "battles long ago," which Admiral Du Pont said that any lieutenant "should be ashamed not to know by heart."

The publication of the *History* was a signal for Cooper's enemies on both sides of the Atlantic to charge on him with redoubled vigor. As it turned out, the points chosen for attack were not, as was supposed, weak, but were impregnable; and they were skilfully defended. The British criticism of greatest importance is that of the *Edinburgh* (April, 1840), speaking rather slightingly of the American navy, and comparing Cooper's work unfavourably with the *Naval History of Great Britain*, by William James, whose book, as well as the *Edinburgh* article, Cooper turned wrong side out in the *Democratic Review* (May and June, 1842). The American criticism bore on Cooper's version of the battle of Lake Erie.

Perry's unparalleled victory in 1813 won for him, as all the world knows, deathless glory. "Furious as the action was," writes Mr. Henry Adams, "a more furious dispute raged over it when

. . . the friends of Perry and of Elliott wrangled over the action." The dispute, stripped of details, turned on whether Elliott, the second in command, whom Perry at first warmly commended and against whom he subsequently preferred charges, did his duty in that action. Cooper, believing that Elliott's alleged "delinquency admitted of many doubts," that "irreparable injustice" had been done him, and that he was a "deeply injured man," after critical examination of a vast mass of conflicting testimony, discarded as unfit for use by a historian everything except what rested on incontrovertible evidence, and, steering clear of the complicated quarrel between the Perry and the Elliott factions, calmly and impartially stated ascertainable facts. While giving full credit to Perry, both in the *History* and afterward in a biography of Perry, he steadily refused to join in the hue and cry of those who hounded Elliott, against whom, for reasons chiefly political which it is needless to specify, popular feeling, especially as uttered in the Whig press, ran high. His sworn foes, thereupon, making common cause with the adherents of Perry, and alleging that he had perverted facts in order, as he puts it, to "glorify Capt. Elliott and lessen Capt. Perry in the public estimation," trained their guns on him.

William A. Duer, ex-president of Columbia College, opened fire in four numbers of the *Commercial Advertiser* (June, 1839), edited by William Leete Stone. He was followed in the *North American Review* (October, 1839) by his nephew by marriage, Lieutenant Alexander Slidell Mackenzie, brother-in-law to Commodore Perry's surviving brother, Captain Matthew Calbraith Perry. At the same time was printed a lecture which Tristam Burges had delivered before the Historical Society of Rhode Island,

Perry's state, exalting Perry at Elliott's expense. A couple of years later appeared Mackenzie's biography of Perry, giving the testimony on Perry's side and suppressing that on Elliott's. Those were the main forces arrayed against Cooper.

It happens that some of his letters which have been preserved give, casually but rather minutely, a clear account of the chief steps he thought proper to take. A few short extracts will suffice to mark important points. "I am getting out a second edition of the History," he writes from Philadelphia in January, 1840, "which is an improvement in many respects, though Lake Erie stands firm. A vast deal of unprincipled opposition has been shown to the book in consequence of the malignancy against Elliott, but it is looking it all down. I have thoroughly examined the affair, and make no doubt that the following are the facts, though you will perceive

I do not touch on the subject in the History." After precisely stating the facts, and rapidly skimming half a dozen other matters, he proceeds: "By the way, I understand Mr. Slidell has been reviewing me in the North American. As might be expected it is all pig tail — on Lake Erie. I think he will feel a paragraph in the Preface of the new edition — if he do not, he must have little sensibility, as its truth is very biting. I am reserving myself for his biography of Perry, when I'll try my hand at reviewing. Rely on it, if they ever draw me out fully on the Lake Erie affair, they'll regret it. I wish to avoid it, but they must not press too hard." In October of the same year he writes from Cooperstown: "I am about to answer Burges, the North American (Mackenzie they tell me), and the Edinburgh Review. I may defer the last, however, for an Introduction to a third volume. It is almost too grave for a newspaper reply, and then it is national. As for Burges, his lecture is contemptible, and I should not deem it worthy of a reply, were it not for the negligent manner in which the world takes up false impressions. I have very little to say to the North American, but it is conclusive. As for the Edinburgh it rests altogether on James, and out of his own mouth will I convict him." At the end of the following February he says: "As soon as the river opens I go to Washington, to procure documents from the Navy Department, for the trial of Mr. Stone,—a libel in the review of Nav. Hist." Going on to speak at length and in some detail of the suits against Benjamin, Webb, and Weed, which, though all on his hands at once, do not seem to have damped his spirits, he incidentally remarks that they "come up to the business with great reluctance. As yet we have prevailed in every trial, motion, or resistance of a motion."

This new suit against Stone, for "gross personal imputations" contained in Duer's articles in the *Commercial Advertiser*, so airily spoken of by Horace Greeley, led ultimately to an arrangement resulting in triumph for Cooper as complete as Perry's: he met the enemy, and they were his. However one may view the "crusade" (as it was misnamed) against the press, of his course in this matter there cannot now be two opinions. It is possible to believe that personal feeling and passion narrowed his outlook and warped his judgment when he was defending his good name; not to believe that in substantiating the statements made in his book he acted with a single eye to truth is impossible. It was a good fight that he fought, an honourable victory that he won.

It happened thus. A decision against Stone on a demurrer brought about a reference of the whole matter in issue to three lawyers—Samuel Steevens, chosen by Cooper; Daniel Lord, Jr., by Stone; Samuel A. Foot, by both. On June 16, 1842, thirty days after the beginning of the arbitration, the referees rendered a decision on the eight points submitted to them, Foot dissenting on certain specified particulars in the second, third, and seventh points. They decided that the plaintiff would be entitled to a verdict in an ordinary suit for libel, that he had fulfilled his duty as a historian, that his narrative of the battle of Lake Erie was true, that it was impartial; that the critic had not fulfilled his duty as a reviewer, that his review was essentially untrue, that it was not impartial; and, finally, that the defendant should publish this decision in New York, Washington, and Albany newspapers.

Cooper's bearing and his brilliant manner of conducting the case have been described by Bryant and by Tuckerman, each of whom was present during part of the proceedings, which lasted five days. Their impressions are confirmed in a long letter of Cooper's to his wife, written at the Globe Hotel, in New York, on the morning after the sittings closed. "The arbitration commenced," he says, "on Monday, at ½-past 4, P.M. I opened in a speech of about two hours. It was generally admitted that the opening was effective. Campbell followed. Then came some witnesses on Tuesday, and a part of Campbell's summing up. He made a very fair speech, concluding it on Wednesday afternoon. Dick came next on the questions of law. After speaking very well for an hour, he was stopped by the arbitrators, who told him they preferred to hear the other side. This was tantamount to saying that his views so far were their own. As they never asked him to resume, we infer that they were with us in the law. Bidwell followed. He commenced about 8 on Wednesday evening, and finished about eight on Thursday, having spoken about five hours, in all. I commenced summing up when Bidwell sat down, and spoke until past ten, when we adjourned. Yesterday, Friday, I resumed at four, and spoke until past ten again. Here the matter rests for the decision.

"At first the papers were studiously silent, and our audiences were respectable, though not large. The opening, however, took, and many attended in expectation of hearing my summing up. On Thursday numbers of Duer's friends appeared, and some twenty of my most active enemies crowded within the bar. Among others, Jordan came and took a seat directly opposite to me, and for three hours, his eyes were riveted on Bidwell. When I rose, he was within six feet of me. For half an hour I could see that his eyes were fastened on my countenance. Then his head dropped and for an hour it was concealed. He could stand it no longer, got up, and went out. Stone's countenance changed, became gloomy, Duer went out, and I had not spoken the two hours, before that set vanished. The impression was decided on Thursday, when I closed, and the next day there was a throng. I now spoke six hours, and all that time, the most profound silence prevailed. I do not believe a soul left the room. When I closed there was a burst of applause that the constable silenced, and a hundred persons crowded round me, two-thirds of whom were strangers. There is not the smallest doubt that we have carried all before us, so far as the impression of the audience was concerned.

"I tell you this, my love, because I know it will give you pleasure. Dick has just come in, and says he has seen the Chief Justice, who tells him that all he has heard speak on the subject, say we have altogether the best of it.

"I am well, but excessively tired, and can only tell you my present movements. . . .

"My last victory over Weed," he cannot help adding, "appears to have stopped his mouth. The tide is unquestionably turning in my favour, and the power of the press cannot look down truth as completely as was thought."

In 1843 Cooper contributed to *Graham's Magazine* a biographical sketch of Perry; and in the same year appeared his *Battle of Lake Erie,* in answer to Burges, Duer, and Mackenzie. Whoever wishes to study the whole subject, including the controversy, may do so in those two publications, which explain it all as Cooper, who probably understood it better than any one else who did not take part in the engagement, saw it. Mackenzie appears to have replied, for Cooper writes in October, 1844: "I am now answering Mackenzie's answer to my pamphlet. . . . He will regret ever making his attack." One who has read Cooper's solemn review of the court-martial which tried Mackenzie for the execution of Spencer can readily believe that.

Courage, as stubborn as Grant's, had won the day. One or two libel suits may have flared fitfully awhile longer before flickering out. They are all forgotten. They do not signify now. The pity of it is that talent so commanding as is shown in everything Cooper did and wrote in connection with the litigations, that character so strong, so pure, should have been spent on matters so immemorable; that the ephemeral should so long have trespassed on the true vocation of the great master of the primeval forest and the enduring sea.

VIII.

BALZAC and Cooper are as unlike as two novelists can be. Yet the Frenchman's article on *The Pathfinder*, which on its appearance less than a year after the *Naval History* he calls "*un beau livre*," is the most sympathetic contemporary estimate of the American, whose works he had "read and re-read." "He owes the high place he holds in modern literature," writes Balzac, as translated by Miss Wormeley, "to two faculties: that of painting the sea and seamen; that of idealizing the magnificent landscapes of America. . . . I feel for his two faculties the admiration Walter Scott felt for them, which is still further deserved by the grandeur, the originality of Leather-Stocking," who is "a statue, a magnificent moral hermaphrodite, born of the savage state and of civilization, who will live as long as literatures last. . . . A little good advice, a little more study and this composition would have had no defect. The navigation of the lake, a delicious miniature, is equal to the finest of Cooper's maritime scenes. . . . Leather-Stocking, under one name or another, dominates all else, here as elsewhere, and more than elsewhere. That figure, so profoundly melancholy, is here in part explained." Those few sentences ripped from their context give but a faint idea of Balzac's abounding enthusiasm, uttered in the ringing words of one great man delighting to honour another by searching out the soul of noble work. Even Cooper's daughter, his kindest critic, who understood him best, praises the idyl of Ontario no more highly than Balzac had done twenty years earlier.

He proceeds to dwell at some length on Cooper's "profound and radical impotence for the comic" as the cause of his inferiority to Scott. That is only half true. Scott has left numerous successful comic figures, and Cooper a few dire failures. But to make that the differential distinction between the two is to contradict what Balzac himself says earlier and later in this same estimate. Does not the fundamental difference rather lie simply in Scott's broader human sympathy, clearly shown by a cursory contrast of his throng of people with Cooper's almost pathetically scanty gathering of men and women who truly live?

Betty Flanagan — to begin with Cooper's first woman — is remembered chiefly as having pleased Miss Edgeworth, for the sketch, though good, is slight. Twenty years later comes Judith Hutter, who, though a memorable character, lacks substance, and fades at the last ineffectually. In the interval appear several pairs of contrasted young women, not specially distinguishable and leaving no definite impression, who all together are not worth Di Vernon.

From Jane Austen's heroines they inherit "sensibility," though they do not swoon so often; but, whereas hers are individual and alive, Cooper's are apt to be mere "utilities." It is fortunate that Cooper's plots do not turn on love, for the feminine element in his novels is totally inadequate to inspire interest. His petticoats, however, colourless and conventional though they be, are less objectionable than some of the preposterous females graduated from the analytic school of fiction, which "murders to dissect," all the while professing to follow Balzac's method of laying bare the heart of woman. They are, at any rate, not clinical cases, but, at worst, thin shades which do little harm beyond trying the reader's patience by arresting the narrative.

It is not necessary to enumerate Scott's live men. Against them stand Harvey Birch; Long Tom, Boltrope, Bunting, Marble, Nightingale, Bob

Yarn, and a few other sea-dogs, each perfectly individual and distinct from every other, and not closely related either to Smollett's or to Marryat's; Uncas, described by Parkman as one of the most attractive characters in *The Last of the Mohicans*, but "not in the least like a real Indian"; Hard-Heart, of whom we should like to see more, and who is in a way an under-study of Uncas; that beguiling, blackguardly rascal, Magua, the best-drawn American Indian in fiction, from moccasin to scalp-lock as tingling with life as Geronimo; both the Admirals, more especially dear old Bluewater; Ishmael Bush, the squatter; Leather-Stocking. The list, which might be made a little longer, but not greatly enriched, shows limited range of character, and few individual instances of keen psychological insight. Cooper opens one of his chapters with the words: "The reader will understand that I offer to his view a shifting panorama." Here we have an inadvertent definition of his almost constant aim—to offer to the reader's view a "shifting panorama," and a fascinating one, to which, as Balzac points out, human portraiture is for the most part subordinated.

The Pathfinder was followed in the autumn of the same year (1840) by *Mercedes of Castile,* which recounts the first voyage of Columbus with, it has been said, "the special knowledge of a seaman, the accuracy of an historian, and with something of the fervour of a poet."

The last written of the *Leather-Stocking* tales, the one we are apt to read first, the delightful *Deerslayer,* which everybody who has once been a boy must rejoice in always, appeared nine months later. "One more book about our little lake!" Cooper had said to his daughter. It is the very soul of the little lake, overflowing with youthful freshness and vivid with stirring adventure. The narrative is rapid, the plot closely knit, the leading character flawlessly drawn, the description of scenery aglow with sympathy. In no other book of Cooper's does the natural background continue throughout in such unbroken accord with the story and the central figure. A scene more suitable for just such a personage as he whose acquaintance we make in this mature masterpiece was never devised. Harmony of place, person, and action, forming the essence of romance, gives to the work enduring artistic validity. Whereas in several of Cooper's novels the cargo is stowed somewhat at random, this story, more than perhaps any of his others, is well ballasted. Even *The Pathfinder*, where the hunter plays the rather incongruous part of lover, is not superior. Indeed, for all its exhilarating variety, the impression it produces is scarcely so clear-cut as that of *The Deerslayer*, which has, together with most of the qualities attributed by Balzac to *The Pathfinder*, its own special virtue of uniformity of tone.

Having doubly crowned the *Leather-Stocking* series with these two books, published when his relations with the press were in a ferment and his creative faculty was incandescent, Cooper presently put to sea again. In his book on England, published in 1837, he had expressed a desire to take a subject "from the teeming and glorious naval history of this country. What a theme this would be for one sufficiently familiar with the sea! An American might well enough do it, too, by carrying the time back anterior to the separation, when the two histories were one. But some of their own seamen will yet bear away the prize, and, although I may envy, I do not begrudge it to them. It is their right, and let them have it." That prize he carried off five years later in *The Two Admirals*, a nobly conceived story of the evolutions of fleets and the attachment of friends, unfortunately intertwined with a ponderously prosy land tale which every reader must wish sunk to the bottom of the sea. The vitality of the marine portion of the book depends on dramatic play of character in such nautical scenes as had never been put in words. Warm friendship between two men of the type we fondly fancy the navy to have been full of before the days of steam is the simple motive. That they are English is immaterial, for Cooper had friends true bred in our own navy, which then possessed no fleet. The book is significant of his loving interest in the profession of his youth, which on some accounts it is a pity he left. For if, instead of venting on his inferiors that fighting instinct which he had straight from his father, he could have given it free play against the enemies of his country, in company on equal terms with men of his own stamp, surely, though we should have lost some novels, he would have been happier. His letters show minute technical knowledge of every detail connected with naval matters; and one can scarcely help suspecting that the words of his old shipmate, Ned Myers, phrase his own frequent, if not habitual, feeling. "I can say conscientiously," writes Ned, "that, were my life to be passed over again, . . . it should be passed in the navy. . . . God bless the flag!"

Wing-and-Wing, a favourite with its author, was suggested by the cruise he made in 1829, in the *Bella Genovese*, along the coast of Italy. The dashing young Raoul, though he may be guilty of half the sins in Leviticus, sails his fascinating craft with consummate skill; and the ease with which she glides in and out among islands and behind promontories is equalled only by Cooper's inerrant instinct in using nautical phrases so as to mean something even to the land-lubber who does not know the lingo. What, for instance, could be better in that way than this sentence: "Instead of pursuing her advantage in this manner, the lugger took in her after-sails, wore short round on her heel, came to the wind to leeward of the felucca, shivered all forward, and luffed up so near what may be called the prize, that the two vessels came together so gently as not to break an egg, as it is termed"? If any testimony is needed to the seamanship, it is given by the down-East fishermen, who are said never to tire of Cooper, but to despise many of his followers because of their bungling misuse of sea terms. So it is in all the sea tales he wrote during the next few years, of which the chief is *Afloat and Ashore* and *Miles Wallingford*, which two are one—with "a good deal of love in part second," he writes, "for the delight of the ladies." His ships are heroically alive; and there is plenty of adventure — some natural, some fantastic, some extravagantly sensational, almost all entertaining. In writing of the sea he could not help being entertaining; for there his heart was, and there, accordingly, was his treasure.

The books subsequent to *Miles Wallingford* scarcely signify, with the single exception of *Satanstoe*, the first of the three "anti-rent" novels. As *Satanstoe* is little known, it is but fair to quote Mr. Lounsbury's opinion that it is "a picture of colonial life and manners in New York during the eighteenth century, such as can be found drawn nowhere else so truthfully and so vividly." One who does not rank it "among the very best of Cooper's stories" may, however, gladly testify to its quaint, old-fashioned charm, and may acknowledge that, despite its disconnectedness, some of the scenes are almost first-rate, and that it is throughout written in high spirits, and without any prosy inculcation of doctrine. So much cannot be said of all the later books, some of which had moral axes to grind, and did it poorly. Of the last, which is about trial by jury, the fitting remark has been made that "the good qualities it has need not be denied; only they are not the good qualities that belong to fiction."

In June, 1850, Cooper, whose familiarity with the stage dates from his friendship with Charles Matthews in the early twenties, mentions having just given Burton a three-act piece "in ridicule of the new notions." Hackett, the comedian, the only great American Falstaff, writes the author a friendly account of the first performance, enclosing a lively notice from the *Express*. "I was at Burton's its first night," he says, "and saw the whole (from the rising of the curtain to the going down of the same upon the third act) of the play.

The first act told exceedingly well ; the second began pretty well, but grew heavy toward the close; and the third act dragged very heavily until the dénouement at the conclusion surprised the attentive into *warm applause*, which awoke and carried along with them in *expression* those who had lapsed into indifference respecting the result. . . . The dialogue was as effective and smart as I can remember. . . . The theatre was only moderately filled the first night, implying a want of curiosity in the public which surprised me; especially as I thought that the things which had preceded it were so many times repeated they must have become stale, and *novelty* be relished. . . . Your piece was exceedingly well acted as well as suitably cast." After three or four performances it was withdrawn, for the sufficient reason that the receipts fell below one hundred dollars.

As the curtain drops on the unsuccessful farce which closes Cooper's career of thirty years as a writer, his daughter has *Rural Hours* almost ready for the press. "It will be out in July," he says. "There is an elegance, purity, knowledge and grace about it, that is scarcely equalled in any book of its character that I know. It will make her *the* Cooper at once. Quite puts her papa's nose out of joint." It is, indeed, an engaging book, throwing a charming side-light on the tranquil activity of Cooper's home life, and on the country pursuits in which he and his family were occupied during and after the period of his fiercest controversy with the world outside. He had bought a farm, which he called "The Chalet," on a hillside overlooking the lake and the village. Thither it was his habit to go daily after his morning writing hours, to superintend the work of clearing and improving the land, extracting stumps, setting out trees, raising crops, and rearing poultry and live stock. The animals knew and followed him, because he was kind to them. His love of farming, outliving his pugnacity, finally prevailed. Tired of the strife in which too much of his energy had been spent, he became steadily more engrossed in the congenial vocation of a country gentleman. He was always warmly affectionate, closely bound to his family, and sincerely religious. His religion deepened with advancing years, and he eventually joined the Church in which his brother-in-law, a man with a genius for goodness, was a bishop. Thus step by step his feet were guided into the way of peace.

IX.

THROUGHOUT those years of seclusion at Cooperstown, varied by frequent visits to New York, he kept up an animated correspondence, showing unflagging interest in national and foreign affairs. Some of his letters express uncommonly sound and just views on the Mexican War and on slavery, and indicate knowledge of naval matters which would have admirably fitted him to be Secretary of the Navy. Long before this period he had written to one of his numerous naval friends: "It is a melancholy fact that there never has been a man competent to rise above the narrow views of those by whom he is surrounded, nor one sufficiently acquainted by practice or gifted by nature to supply the want of such information, in this important office. They have all been politicians of no very great school, or the mere echoes of partisan opinion among the captains. *Reform* is more wanted in your service than in any branch of the government. But the capital blunder of all the Administrations is to have done too much at home, and too little abroad." Many of the letters to members of the family, giving a charming picture of his domestic relations, are too intimate for print. A few extracts from others may serve to show some of his opinions.

On February 1, 1848, he writes: "Has not Scott achieved marvels! Yet his accursed General Order has almost obliterated the recollection of his victories. As a soldier, Wellington is the only man living whose fame can now eclipse his, and Wellington succeeded with vastly greater advantages than those possessed by Scott, after allowing for the difference between Frenchmen and Mexicans." On April 13, 1850, he writes: "Congress is a prodigious humbug, and ever has been. Mr. Calhoun's equilibrium was a humbug, and Mr. Webster's answer another. Still, I think the speech of the latter a very great speech, showing tact, and power, and moderation, and a great deal that is true. It has capital faults, however." A lively account of a trip to Niagara, in the summer of 1850, is followed by an able treatment of the subject of slavery, including this strong paragraph: "A desire for separation is greatly increasing at the north. The present session has added to its force. It might be effected peaceably at first, but war would inevitably follow, as the North West *would* command the mouths of the Mississippi. Abolitionists would arm the slaves, and a servile war would follow. In ten years the whole south would be a pandemonium. The soi-disant patriots of that region are pulling down all these evils on their own heads. We are on the eve of great events. Every week knocks a link out of the chain of the Union. At the next Presidential election it will snap. Tinkering will do no good any longer. A principle must prevail, and that principle will be freedom." A few months later he writes to the same friend, a South Carolinian who, when the war came, remained loyal: "The Southrons are getting into a muss, especially you Carolinians. With a population of less than half of New York town, they talk of fighting Uncle Sam, that long-armed, well-knuckled, hard-fisted old scamp, Uncle Sam."

Much might be quoted illustrative of the buoyancy of disposition, the warm-hearted generosity and hospitality, and the nimble intelligence of this widely misunderstood man. Some of his best traits appear in letters which will never be published. Of high impulses and of uncompromising probity, constructed on a large and ample pattern, "with no more dodge in him," as was said of his friend Lawrence, "than there is in the main-mast," an intrepid, fervid creature who would rather have died than lied, when roused by conduct that he regarded as mean or low, he could no more sit still than he could stop to polish phrases as he wrote. "Quiet to quick bosoms is a hell," was aptly applied to him by Greenough. When affronted, he struck straight from the shoulder. Sometimes he kicked offensive animals contemptuously from his path; they bit him, and the bite rankled. The impetus of contest often carried him away; but his acts, if often wrong, were always above-board; his errors were never petty, his motives never selfish. All this was known to his friends from the first; of late years most people have found out that, whatever may have been his faults, his foibles, and his prejudices, the foundation of his strongly-marked character was valiant manhood.

In the autumn of 1850 Cooper went to New York, returning to Cooperstown in December. "I have gone into dock with my own hulk," he writes, "to be overhauled. Francis says I have congestion of the viscera, liver included, and that I must live low, deplete, and take pills. It was time, for my hands, feet and legs were often as cold as ice, on account of a suspended respiration. I have now some idea what the coldness of death must be. Externally there is no want of heat, in my case; for while I am frozen, my wife tells me my hands, feet and body are absolutely warm.

"The treatment is doing good. You cannot imagine the old lady's delight at getting me under, in the way of food. I get no meat, or next to none, and no great matter in substitutes. This morning, being Xmas, I had a blow-out of oysters, and at dinner it will go hard if I do not get a cut into the turkey and chine; but I have lost pounds, yet I feel strong and am clear headed. I really think I have had a narrow escape, if, indeed, I have escaped."

The following spring he went again to New York, for the last time. On April 8, 1851, Bryant writes to Dana: "Cooper is in town, in ill health. When I saw him last he was in high health and excellent spirits. He has grown thin, and has an ashy instead of a florid complexion."

Increasing feebleness did not dash his spirit. Scarcely knowing what sickness is, he patiently accepted his lot, resolutely dictating parts of a continuation of the *Naval History* after he could no longer write. Beside his placid lake, on a Sunday afternoon in mid-September, as his sixty-second year was closing, came the end of his true and pure life.

X.

NOVELS usually fulfil their destiny by entertaining or boring for a moment before being presently cast aside at a turn in popular caprice: the false and trivial go home to chaos; only the true pass from temporary obscurity to their final reckoning as literature. To build so stanch a craft as shall be borne on the stream of romance past the destructive rapids of whirling literary fashion indicates special power. American prose fiction, young, tentative, sporadic, discontinuous, almost destitute of tradition, often charming for this very freedom, invites, as a whole, rather to irresponsible prediction than to precise appraisal. Among the multifarious species of novel with which the nineteenth century teems, at least one variety, the earliest native to America, bids fair to bloom unwithered in the twentieth — the romance of adventure as represented by *The Red Rover* and *The Deerslayer*.

Leather-Stocking is generally regarded as constituting Cooper's chief title to eminence. So firmly, indeed, has the man without a cross laid hold of popular imagination that Dumas is reported to have taken "perpetual delight" in him; Thackeray, in a "careless rapture," ranks him with Uncle Toby, Sir Roger de Coverley, and Falstaff, and above any one in "Scott's lot"; one patriotic critic finds him "as distinctly a typical product of our border life as Rob Roy is of the forays of the Scottish Highlands or Achilles of the heroic age of Greece"; another calls him "the most complete portrait in fiction"; and Lowell rhymingly predicts that he

> "won't go to oblivion quicker
> Than Adams the parson or Primrose the vicar."

But Cooper's hero is closer akin to Defoe's and to Irving's: safe in the boy's heart, Natty lives with Robinson Crusoe and Rip Van Winkle. Largely for that unique triumph, and partly because most people are landsmen, the world places the *Leather-Stocking* tales at the head of Cooper's work. Taken together, the four books which show Leather-Stocking best — books which permanently enrich literature — probably justify the verdict.

There remains, however, that other branch of the work, where Cooper's supremacy over the boundless domain which he appropriated in 1823 is unchallenged in 1900. Certain scenes in *The Pilot*, in *The Red Rover*, and in *The Two Admirals* — scenes as far beyond the reach of other writers as Homer's battles are beyond the reach of Virgil — raise the pertinent question whether the creator of Leather-Stocking did not, after all, bestow on literature as fair a gift in bringing into prose fiction the eternal romance of the sea.

BIBLIOGRAPHY.

Editions of Cooper are countless. In that published by Messrs. Houghton, Mifflin & Co. Miss Cooper's introductions to the *Leather-Stocking* books and to the sea tales give a good deal of biographical information. The magazine articles and other publications mentioned in the following incomplete list, from which everything controversial is excluded, have each its own interest. (See also Poole's Index.)

I. *Revue Parisienne*, July 25, 1840. Criticism of *The Pathfinder* by Honoré de Balzac; translated into English for the *Knickerbocker Magazine*, January, 1841; translated into better English by Katharine Prescott Wormeley for her *Personal Opinions of Balzac.* (Boston, 1899: Little, Brown & Co.)

II. *North American Review*, January, 1852. Francis Parkman's article has unique interest.

III. MEMORIAL OF JAMES FENIMORE COOPER. (New York, 1852: G. P. Putnam.) Together with various matters relating to the effort to erect a monument, this small volume contains Bryant's priceless *Discourse*. The intervening half-century has produced no estimate of Cooper so good.

IV. HOMES OF AMERICAN AUTHORS. (New York, 1853: G. P. Putnam & Co.) Henry Theodore Tuckerman, who wrote the sketch of Cooper, knew and understood him.

V. *North American Review*, October, 1859. Henry Theodore Tuckerman's opening article gives, with a general review of Cooper's work, a spirited picture of his conduct during the Naval History arbitration.

VI. PAGES AND PICTURES. By Susan Fenimore Cooper. (New York, 1861: W. A. Townsend & Co.) Extracts, illustrations by Darley and others, and "notes relating to the different works whence the pages have been drawn." A beautiful book, as well as a source of authentic biographical information, much of which reappears in the introductions to the novels.

VII. *Appleton's Journal*, August 29, 1874. John Esten Cooke enters a plea for Cooper's Indians.

VIII. JAMES FENIMORE COOPER. By Thomas R. Lounsbury. (*American Men of Letters*. Boston, 1883: Houghton, Mifflin & Co.) The ability shown in this work should give pause to whoever would venture on the same field.

IX. *Atlantic Monthly*, February and October, 1887. "A Glance Backward" and "A Second Glance Backward." By Susan Fenimore Cooper. The first article is virtually an introduction to *The Spy;* the second tells of the life abroad from the summer of 1828 until the summer of 1830.

X. American Lands and Letters, I. By Donald Grant Mitchell. (New York, 1897: Charles Scribner's Sons.) Written with natural ease, from the point of view of an intermediate generation, the pages on Cooper have flavour.

XI. *Dial*, Chicago, February 16, 1897. A sensible reply by D. L. Maulsby to Mark Twain's critical eccentricity in the *North American Review* of July, 1895.

XII. American Bookmen. By M. A. DeWolfe Howe. (New York, 1898: Dodd, Mead & Co.) Includes an attractive appreciation of Cooper.

XIII. Literary Haunts and Homes. By Theodore F. Wolfe. (Philadelphia, 1899: J. B. Lippincott & Co.) The chapter on Cooper is instructive.

XIV. A Literary History of America. By Barrett Wendell. (New York: Charles Scribner's Sons; London: T. Fisher Unwin. 1900.)